EXPERIENCE ——OVER—— DEGREES

THE BLUEPRINT TO GET YOU THE JOB YOUR DEGREE DOESN'T

RISHAV KHANAL
and ALEX STRATHDEE

ISBN: 9781790665747

A special thank you to those who have made the difference in our lives which include but are not limited to: Our parents, our friends, our listeners, our guests, and a few special mentors:

Donna W., Wes B., Matt A., Scott K., Donna R., Stuart M., Brad C., & Christina D.

CONTENTS

Introduction 1

Chapter 1 – Becoming Dynamic 7

Chapter 2 – Set Goals and Decide What's Possible 15

Chapter 3 – Value-Based Networking 23

Chapter 4 – Tangibles 41

Chapter 5 – The Career Fair 75

Chapter 6 – Interviewing 87

Chapter 7 – Salary Negotiation 105

Chapter 8 – Owning the Internship/Job 115

Praise for *Experience Over Degrees* and *Practically Passionate*

"As one of the founders of an IT staffing company, I can legitimately and honestly support the importance of what Alex and Rishav write about in *Experience Over Degrees*. Any student smart enough to read this blueprint will be served well by it and have a serious leg-up over their peers when it comes to getting hired." ~ **Win Sheridan, Founder and Co-CEO of Apex Systems**

෧ ෨

"Rishav and Alex have demonstrated strong instincts in identifying unmet needs within the young professional community. Their passion for mentoring, podcasts, and shining a light on professional development fills an important gap in the early phases of career growth for Gen Z and Millennials." ~ **Brad Casper, CEO of OH Partners**

෧ ෨

"While job search strategies predominantly remain the same, the medium and messengers often need refreshing. Alex and Rishav provide authentic and credible advice that cuts through the clutter. Students are wise to imitate their model." ~ **Stuart Mease, Executive Director of Employer Relations at Wake Forest University**

"I am so impressed with the real-life approach that Rishav and Alex take when producing their relevant and compelling podcasts on job search and workplace topics. It would be a wise career move for college students and young professionals to listen to and embrace the content, tips, and insights presented on each Practically Passionate podcast. ~ **Donna Ratcliffe, Director of Career and Professional Development at Virginia Tech**

About the Authors

Alex's Story

I came to the U.S. when I was eight years old from a farming town in rural Australia and was immediately dumbfounded by the impact of technology on the D.C. region. I knew I had to be part of its progression (When I say dumbfounded, I mean I was even afraid of escalators; luckily this fear no longer haunts me). In an unfamiliar environment, I failed to connect with a lot of peers since my interests have always been different from a young age whether it was trying to start a lawn-mowing business or collecting stray golf balls from a nearby course and reselling them on craigslist. I spent my time in college trying to surround myself with the right people, which inevitably led to the right experiences. I've been able to grow from strong, successful voices in my life and I live to give others who might not be fortunate enough to have access to it, the same experience.

Rishav's Story

Growing up in Kathmandu, Nepal, I can't count the number of times I sat in front of the TV mesmerized by Agent Cody Banks and Home Alone. It was my perception of a "Hollywood America" that enhanced my excitement when moving to the States. However, as I got older, it was tough to fathom the level of apprehension that my mom must have felt when she was traveling to a foreign country with an eight-year-old son.

Economically, we were not wealthy. However, looking back on our journey, I consider myself to have been surrounded with great fortune. I saw my parents work tirelessly to improve my life by utilizing people and technology to foster self-empowerment. The fortune of seeing the value of practical passion and purpose at an early age shaped my thinking to go beyond the norm. This has set my foundation to dream big and achieve the unattainable. As a former food stamp and free lunch recipient, I have lived through the hardships faced by many Americans. The experience of having lived in underrepresented districts and in a third world country gives me the added perspective not shared by many. In fact, it allows me to draw in the voices of those who feel as though they are not heard.

Introduction

"College is the best four years of your life."

Bullshit.

Don't let nay-sayers discourage you. We all know plenty of them, like Chad, College Homecoming After Day-Job who constantly groans about his job, living situation and all the responsibilities he has. He is your basic garden-variety self-loathing individual who constantly reminisces on their college glory days.

But we're not here to point the finger at Chad. How can he reach his true potential if he's not given the blueprint to achieving a desirable post-college experience? In fact, how are you going to avoid becoming Chad yourself if you aren't given the blueprint either? Your degree may get you in the door of some companies, but it does not provide you with a tactical roadmap to choosing the right experiences and then crafting them in a way that gets you hired for the job you want.

What we have done in this book is pull together the very best tips, advice, and techniques for landing a great job right out of college. With tangible blueprints, templates, screenshots, word-for-word networking conversations, along with our personal stories where we utilized these techniques, you now have access to content that you can simply copy and paste and make your own. Whether you were on the Dean's List semester after semester or got mostly B's and C's, the system we present here is the same.

Setting goals, networking, bridging connections, building a personal brand, negotiating salaries and communicating transferable skills aren't taught to us. Either the information is outdated, half of it is missing, or it's all fluff.

Picture this: you're sitting at a college event where they invite recent alumni to discuss professional development for current students. In that moment, are they sharing the tactics behind the ways to network, ways to strengthen a resume, ways to be successful in the workplace? Or are they leaving that conversation incomplete and just telling you to "do it?" On top of that, without diving into the "how," the conversation pivots to passion and how you need to be passionate? When the goal is just to get a job, we're left with no time to prioritize passion.

As much as we fear becoming Chad, we equally hate the conversations surrounding his rival, passion. To a student just trying to maintain a decent GPA and extracurricular activities, it's all fluff. So, for starters, this isn't a book where we berate you like at your family dinner gatherings about applying your collegiate degree or a book that preaches passion without substance. Our goal here is to give you the things you won't learn in your classes, the skills that will get you hired.

If you're an 18-24 year old college student reading this, one of the following stories may sound familiar.

First, there's Fred. He's been pretty average grade-wise for his major but doesn't necessarily see a path to applying it to something he's passionate about. If he takes the time to explore another option, his friends and fellow students will surely pass him in terms of more relevant experience to their industry-specific employers. Fred knows there's an inconsistency between his current path and the one that will get him a job he can be excited about. He's ready to make some changes and knows he's capable of more.

Next, there's Lane, a senior who knows he's running out of time to find a job. Graduation is just three months away, and Lane can't figure out why no one will take a chance on him. He submitted resumes to various places throughout his time in school but has never heard back. He knows how to work as he spent his summers helping out in his parent's local restaurant. No one ever told Lane how to communicate the value of this work to employers in his industry.

Lastly, there's Lindsay. She's never thought about trying a different major and has maintained above-average grades in all her classes. Lindsay now needs a blueprint to get her noticed and accepted by the most dynamic companies making the most impact in the world. She knows this is where she belongs and is going to stop at nothing to get there.

As you can see, it doesn't matter which student you are, what you'll get from this book is the step-by-step path to not becoming Chad, and landing in a passion-based role (that pays you) leaving school that rewards you for you. We apologize if we've offended one of the 270,000+ Chads in the U.S. You too deserve to find a role you cannot only be passionate about but that will pay your bills.

In this book, you'll learn what helped us to achieve the following:

- Interviews with Microsoft, Amazon, Google, Under Armour and many more top Fortune 500 companies

- Multiple offers before graduation

- Jobs we're excited to be at every day

- Working for companies that are at the top of their industries (LinkedIn and 2017 Top Tech IPO, Appian) with above-average pay

- Surrounded by fellow young, intelligent, and passionate young professionals

- Invited to speak at conferences on the topic of becoming a successful young professional

- Personal Networks that include multiple CEOs and young professionals at almost every company and in every industry

- A podcast for young professionals with over 2,000 downloads per month with guests like the CEO of Northrop Grumman and Past President of the Phoenix Suns.

We got here by setting the right goals, learning the employer's perspective, understanding value-based networking and knowing how to tell our stories and talk about our experiences.

What we have prepared is a guide for you to use at each step in your journey towards becoming a successful and purposeful young professional. We've broken the book into eight chapters:

1. Becoming Dynamic

2. Becoming Aware of What Is Possible

3. Value-Based Networking

4. Creating your Three Tangibles

5. The Cattle Call (Career Fairs)

6. Knowing Your Stories (Interviewing)

7. The Power of Now Salary Negotiation

8. Getting Invited Back (Owning the Internship/Job)

With humble beginnings as former lifeguards and door-to-door salesmen, we're now working for the most prized companies in the world. Students who have used our methods have gone on to jobs with Amazon, Ernst & Young, Under Armour, Microsoft, and many other leading firms. The difference between those students and the ones who continue to lag? Immediate action.

We suggest that you first read through this book, become aware of what's in it and determine what you can apply immediately. Remember though that this will be the golden guide for you to reference as you go through your journey. Come back to certain parts of it as you are faced with specific challenges so you can apply the appropriate blueprint and overcome them.

What you do between the ages of 18-24 can set you up to live an incredible life, filled with passion-centered work. College isn't the best four years of your life. If you start now, it's the stepping stone to a better one.

CHAPTER 1

Becoming Dynamic

Sure, she's a nice person, pleasant to be around but you've never really felt the need to chat with her longer than "Hey, how are you?" You've tried to strike up interesting conversations, but she somehow always manages to make it boring. It's not her fault; she just hasn't spent much time learning about anything they might be passionate about.

How do you make sure you're not this person? Become dynamic.

Useless advice: **"Get your dream job."**

Does this scenario sound familiar? You went through high school participating in various organizations, worked odd jobs during the summer, and now you're left scratching your head thinking, how can I possibly convince anybody that working as a parking attendant is directly applicable to the consulting internship I'm hoping to get?

To determine your professional path, you must first define your unique talents. Now, before you get nervous and internally object that you don't have any talents, let's take a step back.

Talent is not a scary word. It's a simple concept made up of three elements: skills, knowledge, and interests. Set aside five minutes without any distractions to ask yourself these questions and at the same time, ask the same set of questions to three people who know you best.

Skills	
Questions for you	**Questions to ask others**
As a child, what things came easily to you?	What are areas where you have said you wish you could do something as well as I can?
What comes easily to you now?	What would you say my natural gifts are?
What qualities have you won awards and recognition for?	How would you praise me to the general public?

Knowledge	
Questions for you	**Questions to ask others**
What topics can you give a 15-minute presentation on?	What topics can I give a presentation on?
When you're bored, what's your go-to activity? (Napping and Netflix don't count)	What subject matter defines me best?
What is the focus of your studies in school or any outside classes you've taken?	What industry/topic have you learned the most about from me?

Interests	
Questions for you	**Questions to ask others**
If money weren't a factor, what would be you doing now?	What kind of topics do I get most excited about?
What project have you pursued or thought about pursuing independently?	In what environment am I the happiest?
When you're working on something you despise, what do you think about to make the task bearable?	What do I spend the most time on?

The combination of the feedback and your own introspective answers have created a framework for defining your talents. Now, assess and analyze the answers to ask yourself one final question:

Is there an accessible market for this talent?

If the answer is no but your goal is to get a job, you definitely need to broaden your horizons and invest elsewhere or find a way to relate your talent to one with an accessible market. Just like you expect your next iPhone to be better than the last one, you need to be better than the next candidate. You have to be dynamic.

All right, the title of this bit is becoming dynamic. What exactly does that mean?

It means being passionate about something, knowing relevant topics, developing skills and having experiences that someone will pay you for down the road. It'll also make you an interesting person who people are drawn to. This is where it all starts, building marketable talents. First, we'll go into how to go about doing it and then we'll move onto learning how to frame your experiences to directly tie into that market. It's going to take convincing just one company to take a chance you to break into this market.

So, what do you need to do?

First, you need to join or start organizations and have an impact. For instance, if you're a college student, you need to join clubs and become a relevant voice. If you didn't go to college, we get it. You don't have access to the same resources as a college student, but that's simply an excuse. Some organizations that young professionals can join outside of universities are the U.S. Chamber of Commerce, National Communication Association, Association for Corporate Growth, Toastmasters International, and Social Media Club.

Although you might think you need to hold a leadership position to make an impact, there are other ways to achieve this. For example, bringing in someone to speak, joining a committee within the organization, learning a little simple VBA in Excel to convert some manual organizational processes into digital ones, you're adding value to that organization. When it comes time to sell yourself, it's all about the employers' ability to see the value you bring to the things you're a part of. Another great way to get a position is to start an organization. If the organization you'd want to join doesn't exist, start it, and congratulations, you're the president! Starting an organization is also a great way to prove yourself as a self-starter. When we get to the tangibles portion, we'll let you know how to sell it, but for now, we'll focus on getting involved in something and providing value.

Alex on Holding Positions

One of my mentors, a VP at a leading software company, still reflects on his time as president of his professional organization as the cornerstone for his ability to lead today.

Organizations are one great way to become dynamic, but there are many more. Here are some additional ways to begin building your talents.

Read or listen to some type of audio content regularly. Getting real here, the average person is on the toilet for almost two hours a week. Break this up across seven days, and you've got 17 minutes a day. Most people we know are on their phones during this time, even if we don't like to admit it. Instead of scrolling through Instagram, replace this with a news outlet. Some examples include WSJ, BBC, TechCrunch, etc. Say you scroll through three different articles in that time, you now have the fuel to be relevant to something in your future.

What do we mean by being relevant? Well, the networking conversation with someone in the field you want to be in is now going to be a lot more interesting. The goal here isn't to have a lot of content to talk about. You don't want to come across as a know-it-all, but you do what to be knowledgeable on a range of topics to be able to ask thoughtful questions. Over time you'll build up an arsenal of knowledge that can be used to engage in someone else's topic of choice, allowing you to show you care, inevitably leading to more memorable conversations and more meaningful relationships.

Another important thing to remember is that everyone will be knowledgeable about one thing. Odds are they will be more knowledgeable than you at that one thing. Take the opportunity to learn that one thing from everyone you engage with. You start realizing how much more, a) your horizons are expanding, and b) people *enjoy* talking to you. Even if you don't agree with them, you'll learn about why they might think the way they do, allowing you to be more thoughtful in your approach to any conversation. The age-old saying could not be truer, there's a reason you have one mouth and two ears.

Now if you're more hygienic than the rest of us and don't use your phone on the toilet, replace music during your commute or at the gym with a podcast. We admit we're a little biased towards *Practically Passionate*, but there are a tons of great podcasts out there. *Sam Harris and the Waking Up Podcast, Pod Save America, 60 minutes*, etc. There are podcasts about everything. *The Pen Addict* is literally two guys talking about various pen products. We're not saying the *Pen Addict Podcast* be the single solution for becoming dynamic, but odds are there's something out there that you're going to find enjoyment in and accomplish this important part of becoming someone people enjoy engaging with. Find something you're passionate about and tune into a little audio stimulation.

Always having a book on hand. Commit to reading it just 20 minutes a night before bed because it's another opportunity to take in new information and up your relevance towards a future situation.

Find a mentor. This advice might sound obvious and if you already understand the importance of finding a mentor, skip this paragraph. If not, well, continue. Now, we don't want to scare you away with the word. A mentor could either be someone with whom you can share your newfound knowledge, including knowledge learned from their own experiences, and build on your own thoughts, or it can be someone you admire based on their behavior and what you've seen them accomplish. It's the hands-on vs. the hero. Hands-on might be the local businessman and hero such as Richard Branson. A word of caution here is that whoever you seek as your mentor will not possess the single source of truth. An exemplary business executive, Wes Bush, shared with us that it is easy to get trapped in a mentor-mentee relationship where the mentee is looking to the mentor for all the answers. If you're looking to someone for answers and you are taking what they are telling you as somehow the absolute truth, what you're going fail to achieve is translating their experiences into what's important for you. You can hear more of this conversation on *Practically Passionate Episode 12 – Young Professional to CEO: A Conversation with the CEO of Northrop Grumman*. We're not shying away from the shameless plug here. We've been told it's an especially useful episode.

Attend either local events and/or events held around campus. Events are great for you to be able to gain knowledge on some topic or learn from someone who's doing what you want to do. Don't just attend the event, though; stand in line to ask a question of the presenter at the end or introduce yourself and grab their contact info.

1. This is a great chance to get comfortable engaging with notable strangers

2. Putting yourself out there and asking a question gives you great low-risk public speaking experience

3. They may be able to put you in contact with 10 other people in their area of expertise and your area of interest

4. Quite obviously, you'll get the question you asked, answered

This is something you could add to your tangibles (Resumes, Cover Letter, etc.) later. *Attended over 20 events on x topic, hearing from industry relevant speakers such as X and Y.* If you're struggling to get your own experiences, this is a way that you can inherit them from someone else.

To summarize becoming dynamic, find initiatives within organizations that you can use your talents to advance, absorb interesting content, have mentors, and keep an eye out for alternate additional mental stimulation such as events going on at your campus.

CHAPTER 2

Set Goals and Decide What's Possible

We look down on the hamster running on its wheel because we feel that we're smarter than it is. We think, look at all that useless energy it's exerting, and getting absolutely nowhere. The funny thing is that without truly taking the time to set the right goals, we're the hamster.

Useless advice: **"Set goals for yourself."**

How you spend your day (Becoming Dynamic) goes into your brain and comes back out as thoughts. Thoughts become actions, and consistent actions become your character. We're not telling you to set goals because you'll put checks in all boxes and successfully complete tasks. We're telling you to set goals so that you're purposeful and precise with what you want and don't want. At some point in this journey, you'll begin to see paths and opportunities entirely, but that will only come from being aware of exactly what it is you want.

The *Boston Business Journal* concluded that almost 90% of people don't write down their goals. Goal-setting is not the same as creating a bucket list. First, take a moment to write everything you have thought about accomplishing. Maybe it's studying abroad, getting that promotion or landing that internship; leave nothing out. The more you write down, the better.

Now that you have written down what you want, we'll turn these into SMART goals. We didn't create the smart goal, but it's definitely worth laying out here. SMART: Specific, Measurable, Attainable, Realistic and Time-Bound. While it is a self-explanatory acronym, people will often define attainable as their current reality. Do not let your current situation limit your view of what's possible. Whether it's a low GPA or not knowing when your next promotion might be, don't let your doubts stand between you and your future. Seriously, we have a good friend who got a job with Microsoft right out of school with a 2.88 GPA and then received a top performer award within the first few months. (Yes, also an episode on our podcast).

Tracking your progress is just as important as creating the goal. A simple way to do this is also to just keep a tally on your whiteboard or a journal that keeps track of how many days in a row you've met your goals. That instant feedback of seeing your progress and the positive feeling associated with it is important for the actual science of forming productive habits. This visual tracking will also help you see just how attainable your goals are and will allow you to make personal adjustments. For more information on the science behind habits, reference *The Power of Habit* by Charles Duhigg.

Now let's get into examples of good and bad goals.

Weak Example of a Goal

"I want to work for a large tech company."

This statement isn't a goal; it's a stated desire. Over time, nothing ever comes of it. I'm sure you've thought of similar statements that go out the window as fast as your New Year's resolutions.

Instead, make this a SMART goal. Keep in mind that for some bigger goals, you'll want to break them down into sub-goals that will help you achieve your higher-level one. This is if the smart goal doesn't point to something you can directly act on tomorrow.

SMART Goal Example

I want to accept a job offer from Microsoft, Apple or Google before graduation by having great tangibles, strong interviewing skills, and building out strong networks at each of those companies.

Example Supporting Goal 1

"I want to build my tangibles by becoming a thought leader in the technology space by studying the content of other thought leaders in the space and then publishing my own content over the next three years so this is an experience I can later write about."

Now, this statement is specific, measurable, and time-bound. In order to make this goal attainable and realistic, you need to create a set of activities that will help you achieve this goal with daily, weekly and monthly tasks.

For example:

Daily Tasks: Read three articles a day from LinkedIn, TechCrunch and the Wall Street Journal to identify trends in this industry: one article during breakfast, lunch and dinner. Keep this habit consistent and you will find yourself reading over 20 articles in just one short week.

Weekly Tasks: Chat for 30 minutes with at least two individuals from the tech industry each. Immediately afterwards, send a follow-up email and always ask, "Based on my interests, is there anyone else you think I should get in touch with? I love sitting down and hearing other people's stories."

Monthly Tasks: Write at least one article describing your take on the tech industry. From reading over 80 articles and engaging in over five hours discussing topics (30 minute meetings x 2 people per week x 4 weeks) related to the industry, I'm sure you have a voice to share in this matter. With a small article that consists of your analysis, you're portraying yourself as a thought leader in this space. What's your differentiating factor? Your perspective is unique because no-one's lived the life you've lived. Now, when you get your interview and they ask, "Tell us about some of your passions," you can state with confidence that you've consistently maintained a blog about the industry.

Example Supporting Goal 2

"I want to prove my value by having greater impact within my organization."

Similar to the statement above, this isn't a goal but rather a meaningless desire. To turn this into a SMART Goal, use this statement instead:

"By the end of this semester, I want to be leading at least one project or initiative outside of my day-to-day member responsibilities."

This statement is specific, measurable and time-bound. In order to make it attainable and realistic, here are some examples of daily, weekly and monthly tasks that can help you achieve this goal.

Daily Tasks: For week one and two, grab lunch with a new person in an area outside of your usual circles to learn about needs and areas of improvement for other parts of the organization based on your talents. In this meeting, extract your value by understanding their shortcomings as well as their successes. Again, questions such as, "What were you struggling with this week?" and "What are problems you see with this company that you think could be solved?" can unearth areas of opportunity to bring to bear your experiences. After the meeting, come up a solution and follow up with the individual. Have a project decided on by Friday of the second week.

Ask questions such as, "What areas of the organization frustrate you? Do you think that if someone spent some time on them, a good solution might be found?"

Weekly Tasks: (after you've decided on your project): Schedule a 30-minute meeting once a week with someone who is leading or heavily involved with the current project or problem. Here, make progress on the project, share your project accomplishments as well as any adjustments in the projects' timeline or strategy.

Monthly Tasks: Attend two conferences or on-campus events related to your organization. This will give you the opportunity to network with like-minded individuals and give you exposure to enhance your personal brand within this area.

By taking the time to write down your goals, you've established yourself as the elite 10%. Understanding what you are looking for in each of these areas will help you when you start researching career options, foster personal growth, and increase your chances of success for any goal you wish to write down.

Alex on Setting Internship Goals

First, not having an internship summer after sophomore year is not the end of the world. I remember seeing two of my closest friends land internships at some of the best brands in the world and felt inadequate in my capabilities as a young professional (Rishav was one of the two). For me, leaving my sophomore year and that summer after with deflated confidence, I wrote down three groups of three companies: three Reach companies, three Average companies, and three Safety companies. If you make a list of companies like this you'll be aware of the names you should be looking for, you can find people on LinkedIn, talk to the right friends' parents, and begin to build your resume for those companies.

Rishav on Proactive Conversations

I remember the conversations I had with one of my best friends about maximizing our value when working inside large corporations. It came down to the idea of being proactive vs. being reactive. The questions we mentioned above are the same ones he applied when engaging in coffee chats or informal interviews to build a solution. Rather than sit and wait to be given a task, the idea of being proactive acted as a catalyst to him presenting solutions on his own after figuring out the person's current needs and challenges. He would follow up with the person with the subject line, "Possible Solution?" and within the body of the email, give an outline of what his solutions offerings include along with an attached meeting invite to continue the conversation.

By taking the time to write down your goals, you've established yourself as the elite 10%. Understanding exactly what you are looking for in each of these areas will help you when you start researching career options, foster personal growth, and increase your chances of success for any person you wish to network with.

CHAPTER 3

Value-Based Networking

Most people see networking as a vending machine. Simply by walking up to the vending machine and pressing the buttons B and then 7, two Reese's cups will magically fall into the retrieval slot.

People who expect to be able to extract value from other people by simply mentioning they want a job are acting like networking exists like this vending machine and all they have to do is press B7. Don't treat people like a vending machine!

Useless advice: **"Connect with recruiters."**

Simply put, networking involves a lot more than engaging in awkward small talk. We love networking but hate talking about the weather. With each interaction, we strive to make real and meaningful conversations. Our success and the success of most savvy networkers comes from a willingness to provide value without entering into the conversation for personal gain. Instead of thinking, "How can this person help me?" ask "How can I help this person?" If you are currently in school or have recently entered the workforce, it's easy to fall into the trap of defining networking as a funnel to solely obtain an internship or a job. Although that may be your goal, you should never be selfish with your intent. Instead, approach these conversations with a genuine level of curiosity and interest to turn your connections into long-lasting relationships.

"I'm young and don't have any professional connections. How do I build one?"

Go network.

We're only kidding. We'll leave this meaningless advice for someone else to share.

"Networking" in its essence occurs in any place, physical or virtual, to share and connect. It is not restricted to a professional setting. With this in mind, an obvious group of people who you might have overlooked in your network are your friends and family. While it may not take as much effort to continue these relationships, take care of this network by being a caring friend and a giving family member. However, it's not enough to just believe it, we must act on these principles to see the results.

The groups of people you can network with are:

- Your Family

- Your Friends

- Group Associations

- Professors

- Recruiters

- LinkedIn Users

Let's dive down into how you'd approach each one.

Family

It's often the most overlooked but easily one of the quickest ways to get started. If you are lucky enough that your mom, dad, aunt, or uncle are the CEO of some Fortune 500 company, don't feel the least bit guilty about utilizing them. This absolutely wasn't our case, but we can promise you that if we had those kinds of connections up front, we would have absolutely utilized them. Don't look down on the personal connections you may have simply because you didn't "earn them." At the end of the day, you're shooting yourself in the foot if you aren't taking advantage of these.

It doesn't hurt to be organized when contacting family. A very simple way of tracking your process is to create a spreadsheet similar to the one below on Google Sheets or Excel. After each call, update the spreadsheet immediately with the details pointed out below (Name, Contact Date, Reason for Contact, Post Call Notes, and Possible Introductions).

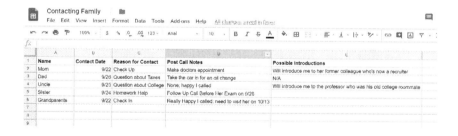

Before you scoff at the example listed, give us a chance to explain. We recognize that it's silly that we've written down the fact that we need to call our moms and dads, but let's face it, what gets measured, gets done. If a small, silly spreadsheet can help us stay organized to provide value to our families, we'll think it's a small price to pay for all the good that's created. The good news here too is that you'll get away with not giving as much value that you might get in return because these are the people who have raised you and grown up with you and instinctually want you to succeed.

Friends

Notice the column, "Possible Introductions." This is for you to introduce them to people or people they've offered to introduce to you. Before making new introductions, ask each individual if they're okay with their information being shared.

Here is a sample email sent to someone to ask for their permission before making the introduction:

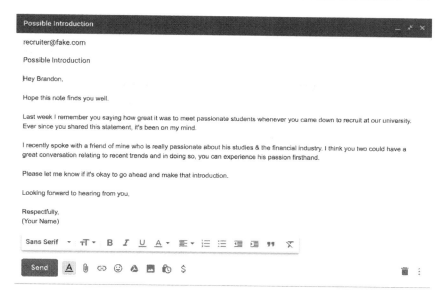

By acting in this process, you have achieved exponential return on this small investment.

With respect to Mike, you have earned Mike's trust and have acted on your principle of being a caring friend. Mike may land this job because of you and your willingness to provide value to others as well. You never know where Mike will end up one day.

With respect to Brandon, not only have you sent a trustworthy candidate his way, but you've also shown that you value Brandon's time by asking for his permission first. It's a step that many fail to take when making introductions.

Once you feel like you've exhausted your list of friends and family, it's time to analyze your associations. These are groups that regularly provide you with the opportunity to gather and learn more about certain areas of interest and cultivate meaningful relationships.

Associations

For this section it's easier to explain through examples, so that's what we'll do through two distinct scenarios.

Scenario 1

Jess is currently an underclassman. Without much experience, she has shown an interest in Business, Philanthropy, and Flag Football. When analyzing her specific associations, she notes all the networking events that happen for her specific areas of interest. In business, Jess is currently a part of the Marketing Club. They meet every Thursday night to discuss the objectives and action items for the organization. She makes it a priority to sit in a different seat for every meeting to talk to as many people as she can knowing they share a similar interest in her field of study. Next, with her interest in philanthropy, Jess has joined an organization on her campus that focuses on charitable actions. Based on her contribution to volunteer her time, she has established a connection with these individuals that share a deep commitment to social impact. Point being, we don't think Jess and her friends are talking much about the weather during these meetings. This means the conversations are of substance, so you won't have to worry about the uncomfortable small talk. With a desire to stay fit and fuel her competitive spirit, Jess has joined an intramural flag football league. With a set schedule that determines practice times, Jess has a regular cadence with her teammates. Using the combination of these different areas of interests, Jess has identified her diverse associations.

When it comes time to apply for internships, Jess now has three groups of individuals she can go to when looking for support in her employment goals. Jess finds out two of her flag football teammates have parents that work for the company she wants an internship with down the road. She asks them if their parents might be willing to have a short call to talk about any advice they might have for her gaining great experience during the semesters between now and her junior year along with learning from their own experiences with the company.

There is a key part to that last sentence, so we'll repeat it. She asks them if their parents might be willing to have a short call to give her advice they might have for her in applying for the position along with learning from their own experiences with the company. She doesn't ask for a job. She's looking to build a connection by valuing their experience and advice. This is key to focus on when networking because it allows people to enjoy getting to share their own experiences with you which will in 99%+ of these cases lead to something more. Like we keep saying, don't harp on just extracting value, *build a relationship* with them. This will also help because they will learn more about you and later on be able to speak more to your character and strengths in the case they decide to refer you.

Scenario 2

Nate is a junior who has held two positions on the school newspaper. He also works for University Food Services to give himself a little spending money for the weekends. Nate has spent time getting close to the people he works with in both of these organizations. He is now looking for an internship for next summer, and through getting to know his co-workers he's found out that two of them previously interned with the company he wants to intern with. They are each now seniors and returning to the same company. Nate asks each one to coffee asking to hear about their experiences there along with how they went about applying. Halfway through the conversation, they each begin to see his passion for the position and offer to put him in contact with the recruiter that helped them get into their positions. They make the introduction and Nate is now one step ahead of the next person in applying for the position since he has inside information on company culture, values, along with interaction with someone from the company other than just an online application form. Nate should, however, not make the mistake that he doesn't need to bring his A-game throughout the rest of the application/interview process.

A great part of these association groups is that the people around you have the same mindset or care about the same things. They might have been in the exact shoes you want to fill, and so now you have a direct peer that you can learn from in a casual setting to put you one step closer to your dream company.

Keep in mind that your peers in your university are excellent places to go for advice, guidance, and connections from like-minded people who know you. Utilize these groups and also return the favor to other members in your group aspiring to the fill the shoes you've walked in. It all goes back to a two-way value relationship.

Professors

Form relationships with your professors by bringing coffee to their office and asking if you can hear about their professional experiences. A lot of times your professors are industry experts with great experience and great stories. If they are from an industry in which you are interested in working, then they can probably introduce you to someone down the road who could hire you or give you valuable advice. They also might know how the tangibles (Resume, LinkedIn, cover letter) should be tailored for the specific industry you are looking to get into. At the very least – and we're not suggesting you become a kiss-ass – the next time you turn in a paper a little late because of the three other exams you had to study for, they might be more willing to listen to your excuse. Make sure that after you've heard their story, you leave a hand-written thank you note under their door. To his amazement, Alex was offered a Teacher's Assistant position just for leaving the physical thank-you note.

Alex on a Surprising Professor Relationship

During my freshman year, I had to write an essay on someone interesting for my communications class, so I reached out to my economics professor who was from Eritrea. It turns out the man started a school as a war prisoner captured by a foreign power. The amount of times I have referenced this story in random conversations are too numerous to count. My world opened to a part of history I wasn't aware of, and the next time I found myself in a conversation about development in Africa, I actually knew what I was talking about.

Recruiters

Recruiters. People tend to think of recruiters as a one and done deal to read your resume and put you through to the interviewer, but the fact is, they're going to be a lot more interested in doing so if you have built a relationship with them ahead of time. For example, if you're a freshman, you should attend campus events that are hosted by the campus recruiters. If you're not a student, use virtual networking as mentioned below.

Send the recruiter a message or a follow- up message (if you first met them in person at an event) and ask to buy them coffee to learn more about them or the company, or send them your resume to get their advice on it. They spend all day looking at resumes, so who better to get suggestions than from the people vetting it themselves? You're disarming them by seeking advice instead of a job.

Here is the actual blueprint for these types of interactions.

With a confident posture, approach the recruiter with a firm handshake and smile politely to radiate positive energy. Here, you will most likely begin your 30-second elevator pitch (we'll dive deeper into creating one in Chapter 6). For the sake of this topic, ask them a powerful question at the end that piques their interest and gets them to talk about themselves. An example would include, "I'm so excited to chat today because I love talking to people in your industry. I'm curious, is your career path typical of most people in your role?" Now as opposed to engaging in a one-way dialogue, you're now conversing in an engaging manner. After they've given their answer, be cognizant that you're not taking time away from other students. Simply respond, "I appreciate your sharing your insights. I want to be respectful of your time here so one last question I have is, 'What excites you about this company moving forward?;" After they've shared their answers, write down a couple of key points to remind yourself of the conversation during your follow-up.

Example

Below is a list of questions that you can ask recruiters during your next company-sponsored event. Simply put, be grateful that they have taken the time out of their day to come chat with students such as yourself. Reflect that appreciation by asking questions that inquire about their paths and pique their interests.

Questions about their career path

- What has your career path been like to-date? Is it typical of most people in your position?

- What kind of education/training did you pursue after you graduated? Additional industry certifications? MBA?

- What trends do you see developing over the next few years in this industry?

- If you could do things all over again, what would you do differently?

Questions about their current position and responsibilities

- What does a typical day in your job look like?

- What do you enjoy the most about your job?

- What skills have you found essential for success in this position?

- Could you tell me about one of the main challenges you face in this position?

- When it's lunch time, what does your activity look like? Are you going out to eat with co-workers, catching up on work, or are you taking this time to yourself to recharge? (This question can be powerful in understanding the company culture)

Closing Questions

- What advice would you have liked to have heard when you were starting out?

- What other fields or jobs would you suggest I research before making a final decision?

- Is there anyone you would recommend I talk to next? When I call them, may I mention that you referred me?

The key to nurturing the relationship with your network is to maintain the relationship you've made. Keep the other person in the loop for any progress or actions you took based on their advice. Also, if you hear a successful story from their end, send a congratulatory note. Lastly, maintain a strong sense of gratitude for their role in your journey.

We both met a Google recruiter at an organization event. We found out months later we had both formed a relationship with the recruiter, but in separate ways.

Rishav on Networking with Sam

After the event, I immediately followed up with Sam on LinkedIn with a personalized invitation. He accepted my invite and I thanked him again for doing so. When an opportunity came to travel to California for an unrelated reason, I sent him advance notice (2+ weeks ahead) asking for an informal coffee chat. I landed in Los Angeles and immediately hopped on a bus for a 9-hour ride to Mountain View, even though the coffee chat was scheduled to be only 30 minutes long. My willingness to go the extra mile showed him my determination and he has been an advocate for my professional journey ever since.

Alex on Networking with Sam

I took the resume approach and just asked him if he wouldn't mind looking over it. This was after he had stated they weren't taking resumes in person but instead guiding the room towards a link where they could drop it. Since I wasn't turning it in for a job and was just asking for feedback on it, the recruiter was disarmed and had no hesitation in taking the hard copy. He gave me a few pointers and I asked, "Based on what you see here, what kind of positions should I apply for?" He said to follow up with an email and that he'd ask a specific team if they're hiring. I followed up and got the rejection. From there, I restated how passionate I was about the chance to work for Google and that I would be interested in interviewing with any other teams as well. He put me in contact with someone specific to the team and I was set for a first-glance with a Google Interviewer.

Virtual Networking

Lastly, building a professional network is not limited to distance. With the power of LinkedIn, you can diversify your network and connect with people all over the world. However, networking doesn't mean reaching out cold to strangers and expecting a response in return. Instead, it is about finding your friends/family, interests, and associations on the platform to extend your scope. We will expand on utilizing LinkedIn in a later chapter, but for the purpose of networking on LinkedIn, we will showcase best practices to identify possible connections. Assuming that you have a rather complete profile, if you want to connect with someone, see the steps below.

Search their name in the field bar and once you find them on the platform, hit the "Connect Button" located underneath their name. There are several advanced filters that you can utilize to seek specific people that correspond to your network which will be covered in later chapters. After you've done so, be sure to click "Add a Note." **DO NOT CLICK "Send now" right away.** Think about it: a stranger wants to connect with you and they didn't even give you a reason. Would you be inclined to accept?

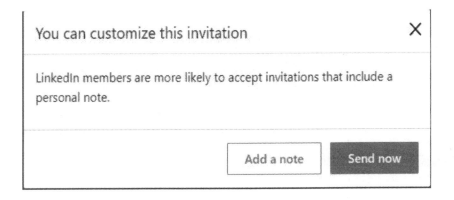

If you're doing this through the LinkedIn app, you have to press "More" which will prompt you to an option that says, "Personalize Invite."

When the message box appears, write a short introductory message that explains your reasoning for wanting to connect.

Rishav Khanal · 8:38 PM
Hey Morgan,

Came across your profile after seeing your amazing accomplishment of bringing new business in such a short time period.

As someone vying to become a sales leader within LinkedIn, I'd love to connect and follow your professional journey.

Best,
Rishav

Morgan Poulsen is now a connection

Your request was accepted! Now, send a follow-up message thanking them for accepting your invite and schedule some time on their calendar to advance the conversation.

Rishav Khanal · 4:51 PM
Thanks for the quick follow up! It's always wonderful getting to know brothers and hearing their unique experiences. If possible, I would love to set aside 30 minutes to chat via Google Hangout or a phone call. Do you have any specific days/times that works best for you for next week?

If all of this hasn't been a good enough reason to go network, think of it this way: society grows from the exchanging of values and ideas. The more people communicate in the world and respect each other, the better off we'll all be. If you're not going to do it for yourself, do it for society.

If you need a guide on how to treat people or even just to confirm in the name of confidence what you think you know about people, read *How to Win Friends and Influence People* by Dale Carnegie.

Alex on Creative Networking

Another great person to network with is, honestly, that person next to you in the elevator.

Alex: (Looking for some details to spark a conversation) "That's a nice pin on your jacket, what's it for?"

Guy in the elevator: Something along the lines of "It's what they give you when you're inducted into the technology hall of fame".

Alex: "I'm sorry, what is it you do?"

Guy in the elevator: "I'm one of the fathers of the internet."

Alex: "I'm sorry for not knowing who you are before this, could I please buy you lunch so that I can learn from your experiences?"

Guy in the elevator: "Come have lunch at Google, where I now work."

The guy in the elevator was Vint Cerf, a Vice President at Google who is credited as one of the fathers of the Internet. Now, did I get a little lucky there? Yes. Would I have gotten lucky if I didn't start conversations with almost anyone who's stuck with me for at least 30 seconds? No. My point here is that you've got to start having conversations with random people. Find some details about them such as their hair, watch, bag, school logo, socks and ask them about it. Again, people love to talk about themselves. Are there going to be people who don't want to talk to you? Of course. Out of the many times I've started conversations with random people, I can only count on one hand the amount of times someone has not been conversational. To build the relationship further, find out what they're passionate about, take down their contact info, and send them articles or headlines you find related to that topic to provide value. This is one easy way to get started. Another is to interact with them if they're a thought leader on any social media platforms.

Rishav on Networking with Purpose

After stumbling on a LinkedIn post written by Braxton Miller (for the college football junkies of the world, yes, it's the same Braxton Miller from Ohio State), I reached out to him. As a current NFL wide receiver, he uses his platform to advocate entrepreneurship, and because of this, I was inspired to reach out. I extended a personalized note and heard back immediately. We're set to have a follow up conversation once the NFL season comes to an end. And yes, this was a cold connection, but I created common ground by stating my desire to connect based on our shared interest in entrepreneurship.

CHAPTER 4

Tangibles

Resumes are like a first date. You put on a little bit of a show. Not in a cocky way, but you make sure to shower that day, maybe you put on some nice clothes, you smile a little more. Why do you do that? You want to come off as someone who's got their shit together. Duh. Your tangibles are your first date with a recruiter. You have to dress up a little. You have to convey your value as someone who's got it all together.

Useless advice: **"Have a great resume."**

Resumes are to some degree subjective. There is no resume that's really going to be the end-all-be-all of one-pagers. It's going to depend entirely on the positions you're applying for and the message you want to convey. Here is an example of that.

Justin is a marketing student, so he's applying for marketing positions. He's going to want to take an approach that establishes him as creative, bold, and unique. He might go with a format that embodies these qualities. This might be an added personal quote, some color changing, maybe something that even just resembles an ad campaign to get across the message that selling is something he's good at. Justin's going to make his resume reflect his ability to create something appealing and eye-catching.

Sarah studies Information Technology. The jobs she is applying for aren't looking to her to have a resume that's super eye-catchy or trendy. They are looking for her coding skills and experience. Here the content is way more important than how eye-catching the resume is. Don't get us wrong, though; appearance is still important for Sarah as well. She just needs to place emphasis on directly articulating her talents and value.

When deciding which resume format to use, don't pick one or the other based on what everyone else is doing. Think about the purpose and messaging you want to convey with your one page.

Sentence Structure

Sentence structure gets its own section due to its importance and relevance to almost every section on your resume. Anywhere that you're explaining what you did, you should use a three-part framework. Say what you did, say what you learned or the skill you utilized, and then wrap it up with the impact/result your work provided to the overall company.

For example:

- Automated a key business process after developing an understanding for the program's financials, using VBA to analyze financial data from four different sources, which allowed the strategy team to more effectively identify and analyze cost variances.

- Promoted to a managerial position within a multi-million-dollar start-up company by conceptualizing and running creating marketing strategies, which improved targeted outreach and led to an increase in the customer base of over 80%.

- Led and managed service projects for a professional business fraternity as VP of Community Service, which led to greater community outreach by developing a partnership impacting more than 100 youths.

- Helped raise customer satisfaction by 20% over a one-month time frame through excellent communication and listening skills to help suit the individual customers' needs.

A key part to this is the numbers. The more numbers, the more evidence. Go back to your past managers and ask them about any numbers regarding customer service, efficiency, profitability, or anything else business-related that you may have had a direct impact on. If you can't get information regarding the outcome, get information regarding what you did. For example, performed customer service for over 200 customers a day. If you worked at a sandwich shop, mention the number of customers that would come in during your shift. Take it a step further and get the average money a customer spent. For example, oversaw $600 worth of customer transactions during a 4-hour shift. What conclusion can someone draw from these two numbers? 200 customers shows you're more likely than someone else to be good with customers now and know how to deal with people. $600 worth of customer transactions means you're trustworthy to handle money and know how to count fast. Even if 200 customers seems average to you, chances are someone else reading your resume doesn't know that (unless they also worked at a Chic-Fil-A in college).

Header Section

Address, name, and contact Info. Don't include two addresses for your home and where you live at school. Have one address, if any. If one of your addresses is close to the position you're applying to, include it. This shows you won't have added stress of moving to a new location on top of starting your new job. It shows you might understand the culture, the people, the way business is done. Also, if the company doesn't provide housing for their interns/employees, then this shows you'll have a place to live. On the contrary, don't include any address at all if the position you're applying for is across the country or on the other side of the world. Today's companies aren't going to be sending you snail mail, and if they do, there will be other places for them to obtain the information, such as the online application you submit. This is a great example about how every single line you place on your resume should be strategic. In the header section, include other obvious things like one phone number, an email address, and a clickable link to your LinkedIn account.

Objective/Profile

Next, the profile section. The worst thing we see people do is write something along the lines of "Looking for an internship in x industry." What a waste of space! This is an opportunity for you to summarize in 1-3 sentences your *why*. If you don't know what your why is, look up *Start With Why* by Simon Sinek on YouTube. Allow this to give you a framework to dig deep and realize the driving forces behind your direction in life. We could write pages and pages about the importance of knowing what's driving you, but that falls outside the purpose of this book.

Alex's is: "An industrious, integrity-driven leader who strives to meet challenges. A student who has demonstrated the ability to turn data into actionable information. A professional with vision of a management and strategic consulting career."

If you don't think you have a strong enough sense of why for this position and wish to focus more on your strengths and experience, that's fine too. Include a profile section if you want to get a strong message across to the recruiter about who you are right off the bat. Just absolutely don't include this section if your intention is to write that you're interested in the position. This is your answer to the gatekeeper's question "Why should I hire you?" Don't make this section too wordy or use buzzwords just for the sake of doing so.

Academic Section

There are many things to consider when it comes to where you should place your academic section. Here's the framework.

- Is your GPA above a 3.5? Yes? Put it at the top.

- Is your university globally known? Yes? Put it at the top.

- Did you rack up scholarships and awards like college students rack up college debt today? Yes? Put it at the top.

- Does the company you're applying to hire heavily from your school? Yes? Put it at the top.

Some include this at the top, some put it at the bottom. Include it at the top if you went to a school with a great network.

It's incredible how far the name of your school can get you with a gatekeeper with the same background. It shows that you'll be more likely to understand each other and share similar experiences and growth. Again, think of the message you want to send by the placement of this section. Objectively speaking, if your school has a great reputation, no matter the size, you'll also probably want it at the top.

If you got your degree from an institution that is not well known, despite its incredible programs that you've been enriched by and where the odds of someone having that in common with you are lower, think about including this section farther down on the page to allow for some of your experiences and skill sets to shine through at the top. We're not saying your university holds any less weight than another; we're just saying that maybe you want the recruiter to be reading about how you led a humanitarian effort first to intrigue them and then still include your school, just lower on the page. What is going to keep the recruiter's eyes on your resume the longest?

The education section is also where you include academic accomplishments such as GPA, Dean's List, Honors Colleges, scholarships, and any other academic-based accomplishments or titles. GPA is another thing to consider in terms of where you put your academic section. If you rocked out grade-wise in school, then yeah, you're going to want this at the top. You should also consider your in-major GPA vs. your overall GPA. If your in-major GPA is better, include this and label it as such. Odds are you're applying for a job based on your major, so they could care less about your intro to geology freshman class. (The exception here, of course, is if Geology was your major). If they want your overall GPA later on, they will ask for it. If you focused on experiences instead in school and have a GPA below

3.3, you should leave your GPA off your resume. This allows you to later explain that because you worked 20 hours a week on top of your regular coursework, you weren't able to spend as much time studying.

Here is one way of listing your educational experience obtained from ResumeGenius.com:

EDUCATION

UNIVERSITY OF GEORGIA, ATHENS, GA
BACHELOR OF SCIENCE IN MARKETING, EXPECTED GRADUATION DEC 2015
* **GPA:** 3.8 / 4.0
* **Relevant Coursework** – Marketing Analytics, Marketing Management, Survey Research, Strategic Internet Marketing, and Integrated Marketing Communications
* **Honors & Awards:** Dean's List, Received third place in UGA's business plan competition
* **Clubs:** UGA Chapter of the American Marketing Association, Mu Kappa Tau

Professional Experience

This is the meat of your resume. Don't think of this just as work you were paid for; ask yourself the following questions.

- What could this experience include?

- Did you personally lead a group that won due to your guidance and contributions?

- Did you take the initiative to refine the responsibilities of a job and create a guide for the next person that allowed a company to operate more efficiently?

- Did you lead a community service initiative that impacted many lives or even change a single one in a major way?

- Did you pay your way through college working a full-time job on top of taking classes?

- Did you overcome something in your life that most people would have encountered and backed down from? Did you sell a couple hundred T-Shirts as a side project?

- Did you manage 20 different neighborhood lawns showing that you're a self-starter?

Don't limit yourself to strictly expressing your value through career-like positions in this section. Anything where you can speak on experience that helps the reader see a transferable skill is valuable.

————————————EXPERIENCE————————————

VIRGINIA TECH HYPERLOOP   Blacksburg, VA
Co-Business Team Lead   January 2017-Present
- Manage a team of 10, developing brand marketing strategies, supervising 30+ corporate relationships and incorporating project management tools such as Asana and Trello to coordinate over 50+ tasks and reduce communication errors
- Responsible for earning $15,000 in 2 weeks to acquire more than $40,000+ in 3 months to finance 100% of the competition expenses for 11 members
- Amplified brand credibility by presenting to 60+ engineers and receiving an award from a Fortune 500 company during National Engineers Week

UNDER ARMOUR   Baltimore, MD
Global Logistics Intern   Summer 2017
- Created a live dashboard in SAP BI that centralized key performance metrics for five U.S. distribution centers, improving operational efficiency and stakeholder management by 60%, resulting in simplifying a complicated data acquisition process for the global logistics analysts to reduce reporting labor by 70%
- Decreased daily data mining labor for a database of 2 million records requiring 60+clicks to 9 refreshable buttons using Visual Basic, reducing the labor by 85%
- Launched the creation of video SOPs, leading to a unified training procedure for more than 100+ supply chain analysts spread out across the U.S.
- Managed more than 70,000+ units in stock and collaborated with 10 members, raising 1.3 million dollars in 4 days to benefit the Heart of American foundation

UNDER ARMOUR   Baltimore, MD
Summer League Rookie (Intern)   Summer 2016
- Developed a workforce development program for a multi-cultural distribution center of 1200 employees and 12+ nationalities, leading to the creation of an in-house computer literacy, workplace safety and a language program to train for entry level positions in HR & Supply Chain Operations
- Authored a 70-page research proposal examining the need to implement a workforce development program that influenced future operational strategy for a new distribution center in Rialto, California

---

The most common misconception is that the experience section is a place to list your day-to-day responsibilities, but what good are those responsibilities if they didn't provide any value?

Furthermore, depending on how much experience you have, as you create this section, save space by not repeating the same transferable skill twice. If you performed two different actions that both exemplify you have a great customer service, they get it, so try to find another talent/skill set that you can communicate to the reader and craft a sentence story around that.

You can list them by relevance, date, or wow-factor. Don't put that that you mowed lawns at the top here just because it was the most recent thing you did. *Whatever is at the top is what you want someone to read first.* If someone's looking over 100 resumes, they are going to be more inclined to keep reading if the most relevant and important experience is at the top. Don't list these in date order by default.

Remember the sentence structure for these. Include the task/action you performed, the talent or skill set you learned or utilized, and the larger impact it had. Let's say you were a previously a Business Development Intern at X Company. In this company, you managed to automate their spreadsheets. In your resume, your experience will be written as follows:

Automated two internal documents through Excel that decreased data mining labor requiring 30+* clicks to 1* refreshable button using Visual Basic, reducing operational labor by 70%*.

To reiterate the framework, by saying you automated two internal documents, you showcased what you did. Next, by showcasing that you decreased data mining labor through Excel, you're highlighting what it did. Lastly, you showed what the results were by saying you reduced operational labor by 70%. Numbers, numbers, and more numbers! These aren't falsified numbers. You should never lie on a resume; it will come back to haunt you. To get your own set of numbers, reverse engineer your hours. For instance, think about how many steps, clicks and waiting time someone had to go through before you automated the document? Count it all and then analyze the reduction in time, clicks and steps your solution provided. Now, you've got your numbers.

Although every professional experience is different, there are many ways to explain how you contributed value to the company. However, sometimes, you may still come up a little bit short. This is the part people fail to acknowledge. You can always go back and ask. To elaborate, give your best shot at writing the professional experience, but now, send an email either to a past colleague, manager or an HR representative from the company. Pick a person with whom you were close within the organization. Make sure they're someone who understands your role and the work you produced. Now, send them an email similar to this one:

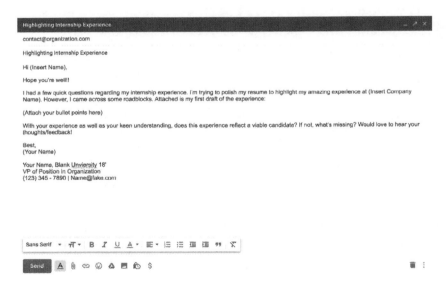

This initiative will provide you with direct feedback from individuals who are in positions where they have most likely seen hundreds of resumes. It will also provide "buy-in" from these individuals when they are called by companies you are interviewing with. They will be able to speak more to what you did during your experience. Lastly, it will provide accuracy in reporting numbers and their impact.

Now a note about those action words you want to use on your resume. To begin your resume, here are categories of action verbs that we obtained from the Muse for you to implement today.

You Led a Project
Planned
Executed
Organized
Coordinated
Produced
Spearheaded

You Brought a Concept to Life
Built
Founded
Formulated
Designed
Developed

You Saved the Organization Time or Money
Reduced
Lessened
Decreased
Conserved
Consolidated
Saved

You Increased Efficiency, Revenue, or Customer Satisfaction

Achieved

Enhanced

Expedited

Maximized

Amplified

You Improved Something

Centralized

Remodeled

Refined

Converted

Clarified

Reformulated

Redesigned

Revolutionized

You Managed a Team

Aligned

Directed

Facilitated

Enabled

Cultivated

You Supported Customers

Advised

Advocated

Coached

Educated

Informed

Problem-solved

You Researched a Project

Analyzed

Evaluated

Measured

Qualified

Calculated

You Communicated a Task

Counseled

Conveyed

Composed

Edited

Promoted

You Achieved Something

Awarded

Attained

Surpassed

Earned

Outperformed

Alex on the Accomplishments Section

One section that has done wonders in terms of showing my value to companies is a separate Awards/Accomplishments section. You may wish to include this or not depending on what you want to do with your resume. All I can say is that, to me, it's been the most impactful part of my resume, and I've heard this from recruiter after recruiter.

This consists of three things where your personal talents and contributions amounted to something larger than yourself. Three points so gravitating that you should even have them bolded. If you have a ton of experience and you want to highlight a few ways across the board that you've really made an impact, include this section. Also make sure not to repeat these three points later on in the professional experience.

Skills/Expertise Section

In this area, highlight the particular skills you possess relative to the job you're applying for. Include a bullet list using 2-3 columns of skills, tools, and expertise that you've developed. Avoid writing paragraphs. To determine the skills you should highlight, take a look at the job description you're applying to and amplify your research by looking at job descriptions for similar positions from other companies.

List skills that you would be comfortable taking a quiz on or being put on the spot in terms of utilizing it. Don't put Excel if you don't know pivot tables or a little VBA. If you know everything about Excel there is to know, put Advanced Excel. On the other side, if you took one java class, put basic java. You definitely want to be honest here. This is a space for you to convey some more of the out-of-the-box skills you come to table with.

Rishav on his skills section

I include this section at the very bottom since I find it to be less impactful than the professional experience I have.

A final note about turning in your resume to online application portals: Many apply online drop boxes will merely scan your resume into their database and are then actioned on by software that tells them how you stack up to others. This means that more than ever, you need verbiage and context that directly relates to the required and preferred skills of the job posting. For online applications, we recommend spending time aligning your accomplishments with the keywords listed on the job description.

LinkedIn

"Isn't Linked-In just Facebook for old people?"

By now you've started to identify your goals, develop your network, and create your resume, but you still lack a digital presence. Specifically, a professional one. I'm sure many people have told you to build a profile on LinkedIn, and you may have one, but chances are, you're not using it to its fullest potential. A recent survey published on AdWeek found that over 70% of companies use social media to screen candidates, and over 92% of recruiters use social media to search for a job candidate. LinkedIn is overwhelmingly a favorite in both studies. To drive this point home, CareerBuilder shares that 57% of employers reported that they were less likely to hire a candidate they couldn't find online. It's not a good idea to ignore your online presence, especially when it's something as globally trafficked as LinkedIn.

LinkedIn vs. Resume

A common question we're asked is the difference between a LinkedIn profile compared to a standard resume. The answer is simple; it's depth. A resume is a straightforward approach to listing your achievements and transferable skills relevant to a position, but your LinkedIn profile is a living version of who you are filled with your interests, experiences, images, videos, volunteer experience, and a chance for someone to directly vouch for you within the recommendation section.

The Basics

After you sign up with your credentials, you'll be prompted to a screen requesting a profile picture as well as a background image. Now, this is where we want you to already separate yourself. Many people leave this section blank. Unfortunately, in doing so, they receive far less views than people who include an image. The picture you select doesn't have to be professional with a full-blown suit/tie attire. A picture of you in portrait mode will suffice! As a side note, try staying away from your Greek organization composites, a cropped picture where you're not in the center of the frame and a poorly edited black and white picture. Ask a friend or even head over to your career services building and ask them to take one! A friendly smile and a well-lit photograph are all you need. Most people will leave the default background as is. However, you can stand out even more using a free, well-built downloaded background image from a Google search of "LinkedIn Background Free Download."

After viewing your profile picture, people will now read your headline. It's the section right underneath the photo, and on most LinkedIn accounts, people will have their job titles or say something akin to "Student at X University." However, your professional headline is a big factor in determining your success of being found in the search results. Take a look at these examples to give you some inspiration:

Marketing at Red University | Aspiring Research Analyst

Student | Aspiring Business Professional

Business Analyst | Changing the Way We Lead

All three of these headlines possess important qualities. They define what they currently do, but more importantly, they describe who they want to become. For instance, "Marketing at Red University" will tell someone that they're currently a Marketing major attending Red University, but it also tells someone that they're specifically passionate about wanting to become a research analyst.

There are two things you can do to write an awesome headline:

1. Think of a headline that answers what you do and who you want to become. Research the headlines of people within your industry. For example, if you're interested in sales, type "sales" in the search bar and select the option to search for people. Look through the pages to get a feel for how people in your industry brand themselves. This advice goes beyond headlines as it can be applied to the entire profile.

2. Your headline is not permanent. Ask your friends, family, and people within your network for feedback. If they don't like it and neither do you, you can always come back and change it!

Now, move on to the summary. This is a section students and young professionals often ignore. Most of the time, it includes either a very broad message or nothing at all! This is an important section to share your career goals, your purpose, and your accomplishments. Think of this section as if you were having a conversation with someone. If you gave them a dull answer, chances are they probably won't hang around. What makes you think they'll do the same with your profile?

The format that we've found the most success with has been defining your first two sentences with your mission. What is your purpose? What is that you wish to do with your collegiate degree? Why are you in your current role? Next, provide a quick snapshot of examples that support your opening statement. Make these short so that even a quick skim can highlight your accomplishments.

After you've done that, write a small paragraph of four or five sentences that highlights your talents as well as any hobbies. Humanize yourself! Think of this summary section from the eye of a recruiter looking at your profile. Would you want to connect with yourself if you were looking for a stellar candidate? Keep at it until you've arrived at saying yes to this question. For inspiration, take a look at Rishav's summary:

The purpose of my work is to help guide our community of young professionals to become more resourceful. I believe that collaboration drives innovation; therefore, I thrive on the opportunity to work with teams to create something valuable.

Examples include:

- Co-host, Creator and Author of *Practically Passionate*

- Led the efforts of changing the way we travel through Hyperloop technologies

- Raised 1.3 million dollars in four days to benefit the Heart of America Foundation

- Former regional manager of a startup that achieved high valuation and a presence across 20 universities in one year

Personal: In my free time, I seek new and uncomfortable experiences. After recently graduating from Virginia Tech (Go Hokies!), I backpacked across Thailand and Nepal for almost a month. In Nepal, I visited schools in underrepresented districts and gave presentations on personal development. Next, with very little regard for proper technique, I have taken a great new interest in boxing as a workout. Lastly, a guilty pleasure of mine includes sporadically watching The Office on Netflix.

If I can be of any service to your needs or you simply just want to chat, please feel free to connect!

The summary includes a mission, a short snapshot of accomplishments that supports the opening statement, a paragraph that is humanizing, and lastly, a welcoming invitation to connect. Once you've written those four or five sentences, right underneath that paragraph, create a section listed as Skills and list your credentials. This will help you appear in relevant search results. A great thing to also add at the bottom of your summary is attach your resume, website or blog. If it is something tangible such as a project you've worked on, click on the attach icon and post it. The summary section is an important part of your LinkedIn profile, so make sure you spend time on it.

Underneath the summary, you will want to attach your work experience. If you're a student, you may not have a ton, but fret not, there are ways to highlight you as a professional. If you do have work experience such as part-time/full time jobs or internships, this is the place to put them. The fields for company name, title and duration are self-explanatory. Much like your resume, the list of achievements underneath is the meat in this section. If you've already created your resume, you could copy those same bullet points and paste it in the experience section. However, you want to add depth to this section. The days of adding your resume bullets are long gone. Instead, craft your story around that experience. For instance, if you had to write a 30-second commercial describing your purpose in that role, what would you say? Create a four or five sentence description for that role right away. In addition to the description, attach any tangibles to this section. Websites, videos, documents, etc. are a perfect fit for this section.

This section isn't just reserved for corporate experience. If you're a student leader within your organization, that's still an experience. Do not hesitate to add it. Furthermore, you can also add volunteer experience below your summary. We suggest that you go down to Add New Profile Section and select Volunteer Experience. The format for describing your experience remains the same.

Below work experience lies your education section. When you first create your profile, it automatically creates an education section because they asked for the school you were attending as well as the years attended. Rather than leave this section minimalistic, if you have a strong GPA, have received scholarships, earned academic awards, or were part of any organizations, definitely include them in this section.

Within the skills and endorsements section, here's your opportunity to validate yourself. What are some key skills that you possess, such as coding languages, business development or other things such as marketing and sales that others can vouch for? These can be the same skills you've listed on your resume. Now, message your family, friends, and the people in your network to endorse you for those skills if they feel like you're deserving of being endorsed. We recommend starting with five to seven skills and over time, removing the ones that don't receive any endorsements. The best way to receive endorsements is to endorse people in your network first and chances are, they will reciprocate. Next, there is an option to turn on the function of being recommended via LinkedIn to be endorsed within your connections. We suggest you keep that on.

Unlike a resume where additional references aren't immediately available, the recommendation section on LinkedIn can take a good profile and turn it into a great one! Think about past colleagues, peers and managers who you've worked personally with that would be willing to provide you with a letter of recommendation on LinkedIn. Once you've narrowed the search, visit their profile and underneath the "More" option, you will see an option to request a recommendation. Fill out the appropriate blanks and always include a personalized note stating why you're seeking a recommendation. A sample message such as this one should do the trick:

Once you've received a recommendation, you've validated your personal brand and have established yourself as a well-rounded professional, especially in the eyes of a recruiter.

To finalize the basics, the last few steps are to customize your public profile settings. First, we highly recommend that you make your account on LinkedIn visible to the public. Unlike Facebook, Instagram, or Twitter, the purpose of LinkedIn is to seek opportunities and maintain relationships. Is that truly possible if you're restricting your accessibility? Furthermore, LinkedIn also allows you to share your profile with your own customized URL. However, a lot of people fail to claim their URL and just leave it be with a random set of strings and numbers. In order to customize your URL, find the section titled, "Edit Public Profile and URL." By clicking on the pencil icon, you'll have the option to change those strings and numbers into a digestible format. My LinkedIn URL is www.linkedin.com/in/rishavkhanal

Build Your LinkedIn Network

Referring back to some of the concepts we covered during Networking, this is when you gather the people in: friends and family, associations, professors, mentors, and industry experts to cultivate your professional network on LinkedIn. Search for their names and send those invitations on their way. Remember to add a note alongside each connection instead of using the generic template. Refer to the networking chapter to see a sample message. Building a professional network isn't all about you. You also need to be willing to connect others, share ideas, content and interact with your network to create a two-way relationship.

There are several ways to connect with individuals on LinkedIn. The most obvious is to search them by name. You can also connect with individuals based on the company they work for. Simply type in the company you either want to work for or you admire and seek out people that you'd like to have a conversation with. Once you find the company's profile, you'll notice a section that says, "See all 50 employees on LinkedIn." Click on that to populate the different list of employees. A word of caution here is these random and generic invitations rarely work. You need to find something in common prior to making the connection for it have a high chance of succeeding in being accepted. This is when you need to utilize the search filters.

If you have narrowed your field of interest in a specific industry, type that into the search bar. For example, if you want to go into sales, type in sales in the search bar. For the moment, let's focus on People to filter on and click the respective icon. You can filter results by Jobs, Content, Companies, Groups, or Schools. As a starting point, filter this area based on location and type in the respective area you either reside in or want to move to. Now, you have a list of people in the area that are focused in your industry and are within your proximity. As you've started to exhaust the list based on locations, move towards filtering your search criteria based on your school. So, you now have a list of people that are in sales, reside in area of interest for you, and either attended or currently attend the same school you do. So much for the cold connection, huh? Once you find someone, send them a quick note about why you would want to connect!

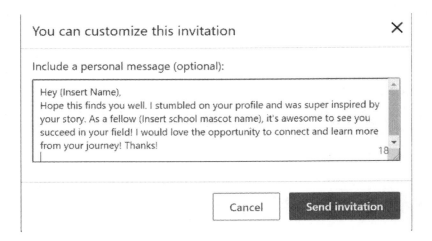

Short and simple. Refer to the networking chapter again to learn how to take this connection and turn it into a relationship.

If you want to expand your network, your school is a powerful association. Simply type in your respective school in the search bar and now, your list will be populated with hundreds of people who attended the same school as you. There will be a section dubbed "See Alumni." Click on the icon to be presented with a list of individuals who are professionals and have something in common with you. Take special advantages of the alumni tool and connect with fellow alumni who your path of interest. This is an extremely effective way to build your network.

If you've either exhausted your alumni network or want to branch outside of the community, one great filter is to seek out specific LinkedIn Groups. These are communities of people who have come together to have meaningful conversations on certain topics. If you're an accounting professional, it may be helpful for you to join an Accounting Group. Type in the name of the group you want to join and up at the top; you'll be presented with the filter criteria's list. Click on more and select Groups. If you need inspiration for groups to join, find a person that you admire and look at their groups. Find one that's relevant to you and send a request right away. These groups can help you establish a professional brand and expand your overall network as well.

Now that you're getting familiarized with building your network, LinkedIn can serve as the perfect tool for seeking job opportunities. If you have a company in mind that you wish to work for, search for their company page by typing in their name and selecting the option that says, "X company in Jobs." This is where you can see current employees that you're connected with and have the option to ask for their referral. The option is intuitive and is located on the right-hand side.

Like we mentioned earlier, LinkedIn is your digital presence. As opposed to always consuming content, provide value to your network by adding to the conversation! Your LinkedIn feed provides you with articles, posts, and insights from other professionals. Including your opinion in a post before blindly sharing the article will yield tremendous benefits for your personal brand. The same goes for commenting on posts as well! Here are a few examples for you to get started:

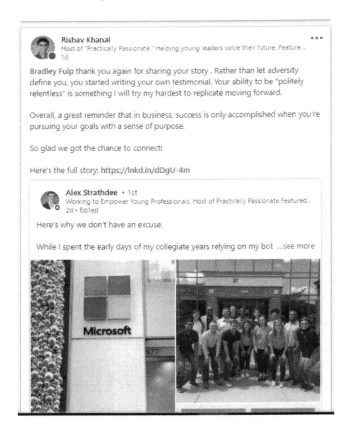

Rishav: Notice here that when I shared Alex's post, I included my own takeaways. These takeaways were brief and concise. However, think about this from the eyes of a recruiter or someone else looking at your profile. What would your guess be on how they perceived your personal brand?

Remember the part we discussed about reading articles, connecting with individuals within your industry, and writing one article per month discussing your insights? The best place to post that article can be on your feed. These are the type of things that will impress potential employers and will help you get noticed.

COVER LETTERS

Cover letters are a way for you to build on the base you've set with your resume. They are becoming less and less relevant but are definitely still used by some organizations. Use this section only if you're asked by a company to provide one. You have the ability to provide a more human sense of your qualities and individuality than you can with a resume. We all dread them since they require so much thought and customization, but if you follow the simple framework laid out below you'll learn why you're actually writing it.

Preparation

Since these need to be customized for the company you're applying for you need to find out more about the job/company. Go to their website and find out what the company's mission and vision are. Find out what their values are.

Let's take Nike as an example. Their mission is... *to bring inspiration and innovation to every athlete in the world.* Their vision is... *to remain the most authentic, connected, and distinctive brand.*

Not every company will have both a mission and a vision, but they will have some section like this, where they talk about what they believe in, what they're trying to do, and the values they hold.

Other values Nike prioritizes taken straight from their website are: innovation, sustainability, global community, diversity, and inclusion.

Now find the position you're applying for and look for the basic and preferred qualifications. Don't shy away from it if you don't have all of the above information; it just means you'll need to make up for it by proving your ability to learn quickly and overcome challenges.

Your purpose in writing this cover letter is to align yourself with this company as much as humanly possible. Find the times in your life that you've exemplified the values they're looking for. Start bullet-pointing some stories for each of their values in your notes. This will also help you write the cover letter and impress them with your interview later on.

For example, Nike values global community so we want to bullet-point some times that we have put that at the forefront of who we are. We'll use some of Alex's experiences.

- Spent a week in the Middle East living with locals gaining a new appreciation and perspective for different lifestyles/value systems.

- Visited over 10 different countries during my time in high school and college, learning that there are so many different ways a society can be set up and that one isn't necessarily entirely better than another.

- Throughout college, every year I invited someone visiting the U.S. for college to my home for Thanksgiving.

As you can see above, start crafting your stories for why you'd be a great fit for the company. Stories can include work, relationships, volunteer work, class projects, or anything else where you've made an impact or grown. Do this for every value they stand for. Also do research regarding recent news releases on the company. Recently Nike started producing a Hijab. Knowing that this ties to their larger values is something you can bring up later and show that you are actively following the initiatives of the company. You're basically going in there with an employee mindset to help you slide right in.

Crafting

A good way to organize the cover letter is to create three sections. The first, short, paragraph should include the position you are applying for along with connecting your why with their why and then follow it up with three main reasons why you'll be a good fit. Then you'll finish with a third paragraph summarizing your main points followed by a final moment-of-courage statement.

First Section

Don't just write that you have skills they want, make bold statements about who you are and how you're going to help them change the world with these talents and passions. For example, "I believe I will be able to utilize my passion for inclusion and diversity to help Nike's brand become one that truly does value athletes from around the world." Come up with three of these statements.

Second Section

Back up the bold statements you've made in the first paragraph. If you've got a lot of strong content to talk about, then divide this into three individual paragraphs, one for each point you plan on making. In your sentences, make sure to include any numbers relevant to what you did. As we mentioned in the resume section, people love to see numbers because it quantifies contribution and helps someone visualize your impact.

Think of a ravine: two enormous sides with a giant gap down the middle. One side is your experience and the other side is what the company is looking for (i.e., their preferred qualifications). Your goal is to build a bridge between their side and yours. That is what your intentions should be with this cover letter and specifically this meaty section. You've got your blanket resume that they've read, which, if you've followed the resume section, gave them a rickety bridge to cross for the time-being. You now want something that more resembles the Sydney Harbor Bridge.

You will do this by expanding on the points you made in your resume. There, you told Nike that you had coached a Little League baseball team back in college. Now talk about how you placed emphasis on teamwork by creating a day-long retreat where the athletes had to overcome physical challenges by working together.

Alex on why you should be inclusive of international students

If this is a job I was applying for and one of my reasons for being a strong fit is the emphasis I've placed in my personal life on being open-minded to other cultures. "Similar to your aim to build a global community, I have focused on being personally enriched through many travels such as spending a week with a Middle Eastern family in the country of Jordan. This is such an important part of my life that I have also made sure to invite foreign students home to spend Thanksgiving with my family every year while I was at school due to the importance and value that I've placed on inclusion of people with different life experiences.

Here's another example of elaborating on something from your resume in your cover letter for company X.

Developed five strategic partnerships with well-positioned organizations to drive growth and presented the value of one of those partnerships on a live TV news broadcast.

Now write about how you not only did this but did it one year into being a part of the organization. Now you're showing that you're someone who doesn't take their time to make an impact. Talk about how you formed the partnership and executed on it along with the transferable skills that helped you do so. Based on the research you've now done on the company, find ways to elaborate on these experiences in a way that conveys that you have exactly what they're looking for.

If this is a position that relies on the ability for you to craft strong relationships, you would restate it something like the following.

I believe I will be able to drive strong partnerships with our clients due to my experience in forming relationships. For example, as a leader of an organization in college, I formed relationships with some of the most influential organizations on campus which allowed our platform to grow by over 1,000 users in one day. I also took further steps to solidify the partnership by creatively reaching out to a local news station which broadcast us on the morning news on the day of one of the joint events we held. It is my ability to work well with people and be creative in doing so that will help your organization set up successful partnerships with influencers.

Write two or three of these types of sections using this framework to prove you're the person for the job.

Third Section

Summarize your two or three reasons for being the right person for the position that you've touched on above. Then, include a sentence that summarizes the impact you'll be able to have and the value you bring to the table. For example:

I believe that due to my experience in forming relationships along with my strong focus and passion for global inclusion, I am in a great position to integrate well with your values of being people-centric and globally inclusive I will be able to make in impact on Company X from day one.

Close with a mention of your resume, your availability for next steps, and express gratitude for their time and consideration. Keep the cover letter to one page and again make sure everything you write has strategic value in influencing the reader.

If you only take away one thing from this conversation, research who they are and tie it to who you are and your ability to be a medication for the hypothetical disease they need cured.

CHAPTER 5

The Career Fair

Think of the career fair as the playoffs of whatever intramural sport you play in college. Why are the playoffs not at the beginning of the season? The answer is obvious; you're not yet the best you can be. You haven't put in the miles, laps, scrimmages, volleys, holes, serves, or practice shots to get you ready to perform optimally. Just as the final game of a sport takes a lot of work beforehand, the career fair requires a lot of strategic actions ahead of time for you to derive value from it. Fifty percent of the work it takes to succeed at a career fair takes place well beforehand. About ten percent happens during the fair itself, and the other forty percent afterward.

Useless advice: **"Make sure to attend the career fair and have your elevator pitch ready."**

If you think career fairs are a waste of time, odds are we won't change your mind. We will, however, state the obvious in terms of what will come from attending them if you do it right.

- Personal contacts at companies that are hiring

- Interviews

- Resume advice

- Confidence

- Knowing what jobs interest you

A career fair is a gold mine for an aspiring young professional.

Preparation

Figure Out Who Will Be There

This career fair is either a local one in your region or at your university. The first step is to figure out who is going. If there is a website, they most likely will have a page about the companies attending. If they don't, wherever you sign up or are invited, there will be a way to contact the organizers. If you can't find the list of companies, reach out directly to the organizers to see who's going.

Now that you know who's participating, come up with the number of companies you want to go for. Somewhere between 10-20 will be the sweet spot. Not less than 10 or the odds are against you, and not more than 20 or you're just spraying and praying.

Research the Companies

In your research, note the job descriptions section and carefully analyze the skills they're seeking. Do you have some of the skills listed? If so, take note of those skills, emphasize them in your elevator speech, and make sure they're listed on your resume.

Next, further your understanding of the companies by researching their company page on LinkedIn and Google. What is their mission? What do they want to look like 10 years from now? Did they acquire a new company? Are they going through a merger? What are the people in this industry talking about?

For companies you really want to work for, research their company page on social media and get a feel for their brand. How do they dress? How do they converse in an online medium? Chances are, companies that have a relaxed culture don't want to speak to you if you come across as someone who's too scripted. To further your understanding even more, take a look at the company's Instagram page. Did they recently go to a baseball game or attend happy hour as a company? Imagine the shock on a recruiter's face when you bring up cultural outings as one of your big values and how excited you were when you saw that the company prides itself in the same category as well.

Now that you've got your list, start an Excel spreadsheet with a few columns.

1. Name of the company

2. Mission and Vision of the company

3. Other values of the company

4. Recent news releases from or about the company

5. Positions the company is currently hiring for

6. A talking point regarding something you have in common with that company

D9	▾	× ✓ *fx*				
	A	B	C	D	E	F
1	Company Name	Mission & Vision	Company Values	Recent news releases	Positions Open	Common company alignments
2	Amazon	Our vision is to be earth's most customer-centric company; to build a place where people can come to find and discover anything they might want to buy online	Customer Obsession. Leaders start with the customer and work backwards. Ownership. Leaders are owners. Invent and Simplify	Amazon Headquarters: https://www.pcmag.com/news/364978/the-impact-of-hq2-amazons-headquarters-by-the-numbers	Account Executive	Share a love for people and putting the customers first i.e. Customer Obsession
3						
4						
5						

Apply Online

Now that you've got your resume and understand the framework for a cover letter. Apply to positions ahead of time. The conversation now changes from "Hi, my name is Sam. What positions are you hiring for?" to "Hi, my name is Sam, and based on my background I think I'd be a great fit for your x role, could you please tell me more about that." It's pretty obvious which greeting is going to elicit a more memorable interaction with the recruiter. We've talked with the heads of recruitment for countless companies and time after time again they will completely reject a candidate no matter their experience or GPA if they didn't take the initiative to at least find out what the company does. There's no reason, especially with all our mobile devices that if you didn't do the legwork up front, you at least can't figure a few things out while standing in line to talk to them. Nonetheless, the easiest way to stand out is by showing intense interest by already having applied for their positions online.

For High-Potential Young Professionals

If you're one of these – which you most likely are if you're reading this book – go so far as to connect with the recruiters on LinkedIn ahead of time. Sometimes you'll be provided with information about who the representatives are, but even if you aren't, you can still use LinkedIn to find the recruiters for that company. If you reach out to one, they should be able to point you in the direction of the recruiter who handles your school or region. Introduce yourself and say that you're looking forward to their presence on campus. You don't need to hold a lengthy conversation with them, but do tell them a little about yourself and that you're looking forward to talking with them more at the fair. This is just another way to stand out and be memorable to them where you already have a connection before stepping up to them at the booth.

Attending the fair

First things first

Have your resumes printed the night before the career fair so that's one less thing to worry about in the morning. In terms of physical presentation, ladies… gentlemen… make sure to have a padfolio and not a folder. You can grab one on amazon for as low as $7 or borrow one from a friend. The more seriously you take yourself, the more seriously they will take you.

Have your plan

Have a couple of "warm-up" companies (please, for your sake, do NOT tell them they are your warm-up companies). Just as you'd warm up your muscles before a sporting event, you should warm yourself up so that you're ready to talk to the companies that matter to you. This will help you adjust to the environment and keep you from freezing up with what you're saying since you've already practiced it a few times.

Then move onto the big ones for you in terms of interest. The entire time you're at the career fair, eyes are on you. Don't be standing in line staring at your phone, unless you're doing last-minute research (which if you've read this far shouldn't be the case). Smile at everyone that goes past and hold your back up straight with your shoulders back. Have a presence about you that the recruiter can feel while talking with the candidate right before you. It's crazy how much of an impact this can have in terms of standing out from the crowd because people don't seem to be comfortable being engaged with their actual environment and not their phone. Unfortunately, this is what our generation is known for so any deviation from the stereotype here is a big win for you – not to mention, the rest of us.

The Elevator Pitch

Now is your time to step up and approach a recruiter. This is where you will introduce yourself and give your 30-second elevator pitch. When you're in the process of outlining your pitch, make your first sentence a great hook! Next, demonstrate your credentials and competencies. Lastly, end on a question that invites them into the conversation.

Example

Hi, how are you? I'm Rishav At the moment you say your name, extend your hand with a smile. Glance at their name tag, introduce yourself and then repeat their name. People love hearing their own name.

Well, John (Insert Your Recruiters Name), I'm really glad we've connected today. As a current student, I've got tremendous amount of excitement for wanting to provide value to an organization that I'm a part of and I'm excited to talk to you as someone who comes from a company that is a leader in providing value to customers on a consistent basis.

I am interested in this industry mainly due to the exposure I've received with my (state a previous internship. If you don't have prior work experience, state how many people or events you've attended relating to the industry in which the company operates). Based on that, I've developed skills in (state the skills that this company is looking for and emphasizes on their job descriptions from your research).

Like I said, John, I'm super-excited to be able to put a face to the company and I was wondering if you could tell me more about YOUR journey. How did you arrive in the role that you're in today?

Short and sweet, and most importantly, you've made it about *them*. Many people believe that a career fair is a chance to show off your skills, but think about it: there are hundreds of kids vomiting their accolades at these recruiters when they're looking for a connection. If you're the one they establish that rapport with, you can talk about yourself all day long in your interview.

After the person you've spoken with answers your question, listen intently. Don't forget to smile, nod a little for acknowledgment, but listen. They might either have a question for you as a rebuttal or they're waiting on you to probe more. Regardless, try to find similarities in their story and yours.

For example, if John answered the question by describing himself as someone who didn't know what they wanted to do, they landed in the industry because they decided to take a chance or they went through a similar process like the one you're currently in, draw parallels! Here's your response, "That's an awesome story. It's funny when you mentioned I completely related to that based on my own (experience x). Now that we've touched base and you've gotten to know that our stories are a little similar, what would your advice be on how I should navigate throughout my professional journey from here on out?"

Similar to Alex's story when connecting with James, asking for advice makes people put their guard down. When they respond, they will either guide you towards a next-day interview or take your resume and put it on the top of the file. Either way, thank them for having a conversation with you!

"John, thanks so much for the advice and for talking to me. I know you've got tons of other awesome students to meet, but how can we stay in touch from here on out? I'd love to put your advice to good use and update you on the progress."

Now, you've received their contact information and you've left a lasting impression. Rinse and repeat until you've exhausted your list.

Following Up

John Haywood in the 12th century said it best. Although he said it the way people in the 12th Century said things, the modern version is, "You can lead a horse to water, but you can't make it drink." What we mean by this idiom is when a recruiter tells you to apply online, go apply online. When they give you their business card, follow up. When they say to connect with them on LinkedIn, connect with them on LinkedIn. Just when you think you're done, the work's just starting! Now comes time for the follow-up. It's a part of the process that many forget about, but a sentence or two in an email can be the deciding factor on whether you get the call back for an interview. Send the follow-up immediately after you've left the career fair so that it is in their inbox right away. Here's an example:

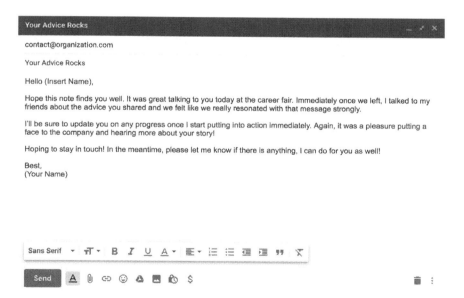

Regardless of whether or not you get a response, you've certainly left an impression. Don't forget to connect with them on LinkedIn as well to follow along their professional journey. No matter the outcome, you never know where they will end up.

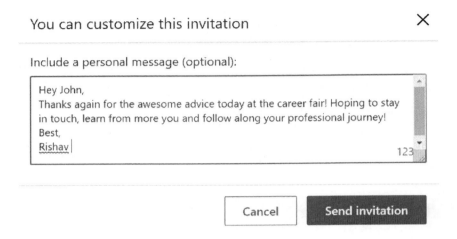

Career fairs are a lot of work. However, in just one day, you've created lifelong, professional connections if you take the extra step in continuing the relationship afterwards.

Some other little bits of advice:

- Don't collect a ton of free swag from companies until the end or you'll come off as unprofessional and unfocused.

- Practice your handshake ahead of time so it's strong and exudes confidence.

- Practice your elevator pitch ahead of time in the mirror or with friends, it'll help reduce nervousness later.

- Smile while the recruiter is talking to you and while you're in line.

- Have a notepad in your padfolio to write notes or directions that the recruiter might give you.

- Remember and repeat the name of the recruiter to them to help with memory so you can use it again at the end when you thank them for their time and say goodbye. Everyone's human and everyone loves feeling important.

- Have some mints while standing in line, no gum, no bad breath.

- Go early so you don't miss the opportunity to talk to your dream company, miss the opportunity for an open interview slot, or catch the recruiter when they're tired and just ready to be done with the day.

- Nametag goes on the left side so that when you shake hands it's easy for the other person to see.

- Attend the career fairs of other colleges within your university or even at other universities if your school doesn't attract as many large companies.

- Give yourself a halftime to go outside, wet your throat, take some notes, and collect yourself.

- Don't take up so much of their time that you keep them from other students. Don't cut them off mid-sentence, but when the conversation is winding down say, "I've greatly enjoyed learning about your experiences and this position. I want to make sure I'm not taking up all of your time, but I definitely look forward to connecting further."

- Many students either outline a generic introduction or approach the recruiter and continuously talk about themselves after the pitch. Instead of making the career fair about you, also make it about the people you meet and go in with the aim to also learn from their experiences.

Congratulations, now you're ready for the fair.

CHAPTER 6

Interviewing

Interviewing is like asking that special someone to your college formal. The other person wants to feel like you want to go with them and they want you to make them feel uniquely special. The same goes for interviews. Giving generic answers will not make it memorable for anyone involved. To make it personable and relatable, it's simple: do your homework. We're sure you get the point by now that research is half the battle.

Useless advice: **"Do your research and make sure to practice."**

Behavioral

Interview Prep

Know the company's industry, problems, and initiatives. For every interview we've gone into, we've had some sort of tangible to compile our research and our thoughts on it. A good way to do this is with a PowerPoint. Each slide covers information relating to some other portion of the company. If you already did your research on the company from your career fair, this will be a good place to work off of but now you need to go deeper.

- Title slide: Name of Company and position(s) you're interviewing for.

- Slide 2: Mission, Vision, and Values of the company.

- Slide 3: Headlines on recent company news with links to the articles or screenshot them onto multiple slides.

- Slide 4: The company's product/service offering (You should obviously know what people pay them for).

- Slide 5: The company's industry. Is it growing or shrinking? Who are the competitors? What do they do better?

- Slide 6: Primary and secondary contacts at the company.

- Slide 7: Other information such as size, revenue, key leaders.

Answering these questions is a great way to understanding the core reason why executive leaders started the business or evolved it into what it is today. Now, where do you find the information? Obviously, the company website is a great place to start, and should have tabs/pages about the company. If it's a publicly-traded company, read their recent shareholder letter. A shareholder letter is written by executives to its shareholders to provide a broad overview of the business throughout the year. The shareholder letter will contain key areas of focus for the organization.

Google the company and attach the phrase "first-round interview" to the search box. Example: "First Round Interview with KPMG." Sometimes, sites like Glassdoor will have questions that other people were asked, and it can give you a good framework for the type of questions you should expect. While you're online, search the company pages on LinkedIn. Do you have any connections that currently work there? If so, shoot them a message similar to the one below:

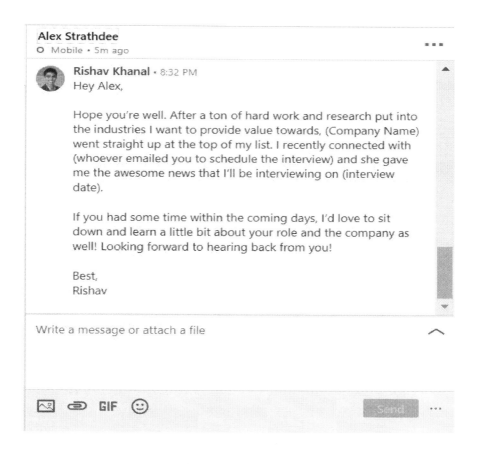

Practice: We've heard from countless colleagues who lost an interview because they were so nervous. Although on the inside you might still feel like a wreck, you have to get to a point where this is where it stays, on the inside. The way you often believe you're acting in stressful situations is not necessarily how someone perceives you. Remember this the next time you're stressed out in an interview. Just knowing nervousness is something you can learn to hide will help calm you down.

So, how do you get to the point where the interviewer perceives you as being confident? Practice, Practice, Practice. We're going to take you through the top 10 questions on the next page. Know your answers inside and out, and by that we mean your stories which we'll get to in the question part. If you have your 5-6 stories of times where you've put your value on display, then you can frame them to answer any question. Once you know your stories, and therefore your answers, that's one less thing that can go wrong.

Find a friend, professor or parents and have them ask you questions on end for an hour or two. A lot of our friends will tell you that we've spent hours getting drilled with questions from them, and we asked for it. Once you become so comfortable with it, the interviewer will only be halfway through the question, and you'll already know your go-to story and how to frame it towards the question being asked. Obviously, this doesn't mean cut them off half way through their question.

Now comes time to tackle the actual interview. Listed below are some common interview questions you'll be asked. The answers below will give you the framework to write your own story and crush it from there!

So, tell me about yourself.

How you answer this question sets the tone for the entire interview. This question isn't about you on a day-to-day level, but more about your professional brand. Similar to your elevator pitch, you need to have a hook that talks about something you value that the company values as well. (You now know their values thanks to your research). Next, you provide an example that validates your initial point and afterwards, you end your answer with a crisp sentence that ties it all together.

Alex's response:

I came to the U.S. at the age of eight from a small farming town in Australia and was immediately inspired by the impact of technology in the D.C. region. I knew I had to be a part of it. Throughout high school, I explored many facets of life by joining different organizations which led to my time at Virginia Tech studying Technologies relevance to business. Here I began to cultivate a habit of being involved in industry-related organizations where I could develop necessary skills, talents, and interests that I could bring into the workforce. My greatest growth came from holding multiple positions within these different organizations and the initiatives I was able to take charge of in those respective positions. I want to bring this experience to have an impact as a X for your company.

How has your experience prepared you for this role?

There is a great way to reverse-engineer this question based on your research. Often, the job posting will include a qualifications and skills section. They will highlight areas such as communication, decision-making, and others. People may consider this segment to be fluffy, but if you showcase that you exhibit the qualities that they're seeking for based on your experiences, your chances increase that much more.

Rishav's answer:

Certainly! I believe I possess a unique set of experiences that align well with this position. My understanding of this role is that you're seeking a candidate who is analytical and possesses strong decision-making skills. During my internship, I was responsible for analyzing the firm's operational efficiency and as opposed to providing just a static product, I created a live dashboard that assesses the company against its own internal benchmarks by analyzing it across key performance metrics to distribute to the executive stakeholders. The result in simplifying and consolidating the labor improved internal efficiency by 60% and increased overall executive-viewpoint of the business. My analytical and strong decision-making skills give me the opportunity to not only understand why certain practices exist, but also create a way to conduct those best practices in a workplace setting. Therefore, I believe my actions are purposeful and my experiences fit this role well.

Notice that the last sentence restates the question and gives the interviewer the feel that you've answered the question completely.

Why are you interested in this position/our company?

Do not talk about the company's reputation, but rather talk about what the company's values and its actions represent on a larger scale. Open yourself up to vulnerabilities here. Everyone wants a job, but why do you want this one? Make your actions purposeful and align your actions with the company's values.

Rishav's Answer:

First, my interest in this field hits really close to home. Economically, we were not wealthy when my mom and I immigrated to the states in 2006. However, looking back on our journey, I consider myself to have been surrounded with great fortune. I saw my parents work tirelessly to improve my life by utilizing technology to foster self-empowerment. Therefore, I owe my source of inspiration of wanting to change the world and believe the impossible to my parents. And through LinkedIn's 500 million and growing user base, a goal to empower the three billion people of the global workforce and the mission to connect talent with opportunity, the thought of changing the world becomes a clear objective.

What is your biggest weakness?

This question isn't a tough question. However, where most fail to turn this question into an easy win is when they just dwell on the negative as opposed sharing how they're improving in these areas to make themselves better.

Alex's answer:

My biggest weakness is that I get terribly anxious whenever I have to present in front of more than two other people. I get sickly nervous, my palms sweat, I stutter, I imagine the worst. I knew the only way to get over this was to walk through the ring of fire itself. I signed up to be the TA of a 550-person class where I would have to speak in front of large crowds. I came to realize the trick is to do it as many times a possible until I was comfortable. Further, I realized that the more I practiced ahead of time, and knew my presentation's content, the less that could go wrong. I put myself in situations where I was forced to face my fear and although I still sometimes get nervous before speaking, the people I'm speaking to never know it.

Tell me about a time you worked with a group.

What they're looking for here is communication skills and accountability. Provide a time you communicated well by listening more than talking. Also make sure it was a time there was a measurable impact, whether it be a grade or an award, and your direct impact on that outcome.

Alex's Answer:

We were given the role of consultant for helping an organization achieve their goals. We chose the Athletic department to build out a VBA platform to help schedule tutors with their athletes. I volunteered to be the project manager due to how I felt I could best contribute with my organization skills and ability to work with people to get outcomes. By listening to the struggles of various team members, finding where they could contribute best, along with making sure we were pacing ourselves throughout the semester, we were able to receive an A grade on the project and made our project sponsor, who was the director of the Student Athlete Support Division, very appreciative and thankful.

Tell me about a time you had a disagreement with someone.

What they're looking for here are your conflict-resolution skills. It's okay to admit you were wrong in your approach to whatever situation you bring up as long as you follow it up with solutions on how you've moved forward.

Rishav's answer:

Yeah, certainly! No one favors disagreements outright, but I do value those conversations because I find a lot of good to come out of them when they're conducted properly. For instance, when working on creating an email campaign to send to our list of over 500 external customers, my colleague and I disagreed on the content of the email. Instead of entering into the conversation with the intention to win, I asked questions such as, "What is our objective?" "Based on your experience, why do you feel like this content adheres to the intended objective? and what does success look like to you?" We answered the questions and found that our objective for the campaign differed and addressed the root cause of the problem to make sure we were in alignment. Furthermore, we worked together to create three options to send our internal team a survey to assess our content. One was mine, one was his and the other content was something we worked on together based on our findings. It turns that our internal team favored my colleagues' content, but the larger success story is that we created a framework for a larger collaboration with the team as well as guiding our actions to always refer back to our original objective.

Tell us about a time you overcame a problem.

Think of a time when you faced a difficult life problem. How did you handle it? It's similar to a college math exam and the professor says to "show your work." The reason he says that is because he wants to see your thinking process when it comes to challenges.

Alex's Answer:

My senior year I took on an executive role within my organization because I saw a flaw in the way our organization trained new members. I had heard many discuss their frustrations with the process and knew that this was a problem that needed solving. I formulated a plan by reading books about personal development and created activities and events that reflected what I learned. I still get thank you notes today from the people I brought into the organization for the personal development they received. I saw a problem, took on the role of the person who was going to fix it and implemented the solution.

What is your greatest strength?

It's pretty simple here. They want to know what your big value proposition is.

Rishav's answer:

I believe my ability to work with teams to create something unique is my greatest strength. I attribute this success towards my ability to recognize the team's strength and recognize the areas where I can provide value for the betterment of our objective. For one weekend, I was tasked to manage a self-pop up store for Under Armour all within one week by renting out an old space that previously used to be a building owned by Walmart. A week prior, I attended meetings with the leadership team to discover everyone's strength and comfort factor and that resulted in tremendous value during the days of the sale. I was in charge of managing more than 70,000+ units in stock and collaborated with 10 members which resulted in raising 1.3 million dollars in four days to benefit the Heart of America foundation.

Tell us about any leadership experience.

Don't think the only thing you can include here is a leadership title such as President or Vice President for a club or group. Have you ever led a group of friends, a project or something in your life where you've made a decision and it has created positive results? The organization wants someone who will be a leader within their organization and has experience in this area.

Alex's approach:

Like we mentioned, these questions are all about knowing your stories. If I have not previously used my project management as a story yet, I could also tie in the project management class project where we created a VBA platform to assist the student athlete services division. Not only did I work in a group in that situation, but I also lead the group. For the answer now I would focus on how I placed emphasis on strong communications and making sure everyone was clear on expectations. Like we mentioned above, this is why we encourage you to know five or six times when you've shown your talents and overcame challenges and build out stories around those. From there you can answer any question that comes your way simply by framing it to suit the interviewer's questions.

Do you have any questions for us?

Say you have three good questions. Based on your research about the company, ask two thoughtful questions that apply to your position or the company.

Example: Why does your company perform X process instead of Y, which the rest of the industry follows? What does the development of X technology mean for the future of your Y division?

Then for the third question, say that it's actually a comment instead. What you're going to say is known as a moment of courage.

You must cut out the political correctness for at least 30 seconds of the interview to truly show who you are. Say there is something I want you to know about me. This is when you let it go. You find something from your life that has really shaped you. Typically, it's a circumstance and its extremely personal. You pretty much say when I was X years old, Y happened to me. Ever since then I wake up every single day with a fire inside of me that is stronger than the next five people you will meet. Because of Y, I can guarantee you that I'm the person that will take your company to the next level.

Lastly, how to answer a question you don't know the answer to:

For any question relating to actual knowledge of processes or industry relevant information that you don't know, it's ACTUALLY OKAY to admit that you don't know. Just make sure to follow it up with the fact that you're willing to learn and have time and time again, learned very quickly on the job. They want to see that you're willing to put aside your ego to learn what needs to be learned.

Interview Day

The 30 Rule

Make sure that you know ahead of time how long it's going to take to travel to your interview. If your interview is on a Friday morning, check the traffic on the Friday before at that time for the route you will be travelling. Waze also has a feature that tells you how long you can expect to be held up if you travel at a certain time.

Plan on getting to the parking lot 30 minutes before your interview and make sure to be in the building 15 minutes prior to the interview start time. The first 15 minutes will give you time in case something goes wrong traveling there. If nothing goes wrong and you're there early, pull up your research PowerPoint and review it one last time. The other extra 15 minutes is in case you have trouble parking or actually finding the place you're supposed to be. At a campus like Microsoft, it might take you 15 minutes just to find the right building.

Smile at everyone and introduce yourself first

From the receptionist to the janitor to the other candidates… smile. Only good things can come from having an expression on your face that shows excitement for where you are. The interviewers will notice that you have a presence that lifts the place up. They don't want to hire someone in a crappy mood. Next, we're all afraid that if we extend an open hand to someone else, we'll face rejection. It's honestly the downfall of humanity. Especially if it's a client-facing role you're vying for, the company wants to see that you are focused on forming relationships with anyone and everyone. Another reason you should be introducing yourself to everyone including other candidates is because of the networking aspect.

Think about it this way. All of the people at this interview are individuals who have been chosen by the company that also chose you and therefore are also successful individuals. You don't know where these people will end up, but odds are it's going to be a success story.

Alex on Bradley Fulp

I met a guy named Bradley Fulp at my interview. We ended up connecting on a very personal level due to our passions and we've stayed in touch since. He went on to work for Microsoft, and I have no doubt he will one day be helping to run the company. On top of this, he has such a great story of overcoming adversity that we brought him on our podcast to talk about how he graduated with a 2.88 GPA and still got hired by Microsoft right out of undergrad.

Interviews are a great place to meet incredible individuals and make lifelong connections; so take the initiative to introduce yourself first. A good question to always lead with is "Hi, I'm Alex, where are you from?"

Body language

Verbal and non-verbal, the whole package. You've got your answers nailed but you still need to exude confidence when sharing them. Keep a sharp posture, back up straight, shoulders back. Again, it's about the presence. Keep your hands in plain sight because it shows you've got nothing to hide.

Okay, so interview day has come to an end, you get back to wherever you're sleeping that night. Open your laptop and send thank-you emails to everyone you met, not just the people who interviewed you. This also means you should ask for a business card from employees you meet throughout the day or who are acting as ushers for the campus interviews along with any of the recruiters you also encountered on the day. Here is an example.

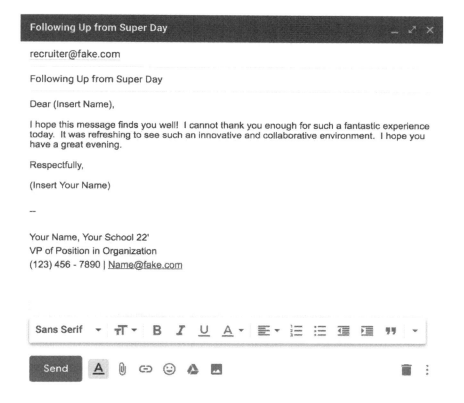

It's also okay to follow up again five to seven days after the first email if they haven't gotten back to you on a decision yet. It shows you are still interested in the role. Check out the simple email template obtained from Indeed:

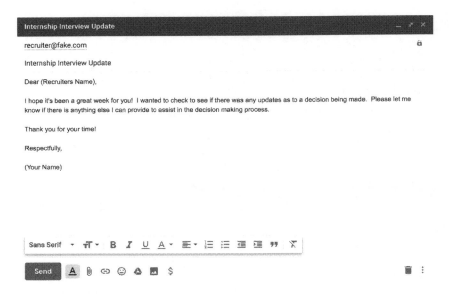

They will probably get back to you with something like, "Our apologies for the delay, we appreciate your excitement for the position and will make sure to get back to you within five business days on our decision." You may also wish to write a formal thank you card to them but since snail mail is inherently slow, you do want to get them a thank-you message before they make their decision on you. A way you can overcome this is also by having thank you cards written in advance, except for the "Dear So and So." Then, you can just add in a name, and maybe a sentence at the end regarding a personal bit of information you talked about such as their experience. As soon as the interview is over and you're back in the lobby, add in these personalized bits quickly and go back and hand them to the interviewers or if they're busy, someone else who can get it to them later.

They Get Back with a Yes

Great, now to ask for feedback and ways you can improve. This will help them know they've made the right choice with someone who's focused on growth. Showing this value early on can help as soon as the salary negotiation.

They Get Back with a No

Don't take no for an answer.

Alex on Not Accepting the Rejection

I was rejected for an internship with a consulting company my junior year. I had developed (thanks to networking) a relationship with a partner at the firm, so when I was rejected for one position, I reached back out to him asking about the opportunity to interview for another position. He reached out to the department that rejected me who had only good things to say other than a few questions I hadn't done too well in and got back to me with an invitation for a different department. This time, I got an offer.

CHAPTER 7

Salary Negotiation

Salary negotiation is like being upset at a professor after you came so close to getting that grade. Did you ask if you could get the small bump you need? Sure, it was outlined that a final grade is a final grade, but have you done your analysis of why you think you deserve the bump based on your prior work history in the class? Maybe if you develop a strong case for it, you might get it. It's always a no if you don't ask. The same goes for salary negotiations.

Useless advice: **"You should ask for a higher salary."**

The apprehension that stems from being a young professional with limited experience is a common fear, but it's a bad misconception. The fact is that employers do not perceive your initiative to negotiate as selfish, but as a capable employee that knows their worth. NerdWallet estimates that just 38% of recent graduates negotiate their salary upon receiving the offer despite three-quarters of employers saying that they typically have room to increase their first-year offer by 5-10%. You will never get something if you don't ask for it. Negotiation is not a zero-sum game. Business is about relationships and providing value to all parties involved. Negotiation falls nicely under this umbrella as a conversation when articulated with polite, non-combative dialogue can benefit all parties involved.

In order to understand the negotiation process, you have to understand your worth to the overall market. There are two factors to this: your individual worth vs. your external worth. Your individual worth is defined as your talents and potential as an individual. This is your unique selling proposition in the negotiation process. For instance, if you're an intern or a full-time professional and have a specialized skill such as knowing a specific software or language and no one else in the company has this knowledge, this would be your specialized skill. To determine your worth as an individual within the market, ask yourself how do my prior accomplishments, talents, and previous work experience contribute value to this position? If you're still a little stuck to determine your accomplishments, you'll want to consider things such as awards, professional certifications, measurable positive results from your leadership roles, skills where you particularly excel, and contributions you've made towards a project or an outcome to help you establish that list.

Once you've made your list of accomplishments, extrapolate on the action and talk about what you did to make it happen. Next, use this template that we developed after attending a smart salary negotiation workshop to express your value when making your case for why you're worthy to have the conversation to begin with:

As a result of _____ (List a specific action) during my time with Company X, I have achieved _____ (The result from the action), which provided the company with _____ (Benefits that company/organization accumulated from your result). Therefore, I'd love to discuss my opportunity for the future in providing additional value and having that be reflected in my compensation package.

Example: As a result of spearheading sales and marketing, I have achieved the highest response rate in the company's history for the annual event, which provided the company with a guarantee that the event's total attendance would increase by 30%. Therefore, I'd love to discuss my opportunity for the future in providing additional value and having that reflected in my compensation package.

Your external worth is based on looking outside your company and analyzing the industry as a whole. What is an intern or a full-time professional earning in their company compared to what you're currently being offered? Knowing these considerations will help you research and determine the strategies to increase your base pay.

To gather a realistic data of what the market pays, visit the Bureau of Labor Statistics (https://www.bls.gov/), one of the most reliable source of job data. Now, once you're on the home page, you'll want to go under "Subjects" and click on "Wages by Area and Occupation."

Here, you'll select "For over 800 occupations" and be prompted to select an occupational category that best suits your scenario. In this example, we will select "Business and Financial Operations Occupations." You'll now see a table and will be required to select an Occupation title. Select a title that best suits you and for this example, we will select "Financial Analysts."

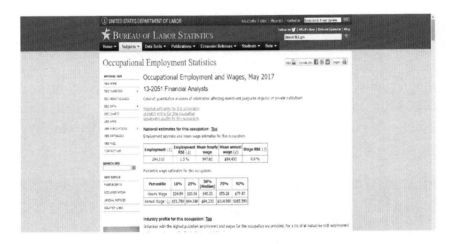

You can see a breakdown of the annual wage as well as the hourly rate for the position. However, don't let this number guide you as the single source of truth. There are many factors to assess when you're finding your external equity such as overall economic conditions of your area, the company's financial health as well as special conditions within your particular industry to name a few. Therefore, dive into the research a little bit more and break down your specific value based on the state you plan to work in by scrolling down on the website and analyzing the statistic further.

Delaware	3,530	7.47	3.86	$41.54	$86,460
New York	52,670	5.72	2.77	$64.89	$134,963
District of Columbia	3,260	4.74	2.30	$50.41	$104,863
Connecticut	5,900	3.57	1.73	$52.32	$108,820
Massachusetts	11,750	3.31	1.61	$46.97	$97,696

Annual mean wage of financial analysts, by state, May 2017

Here, you can hover over the state and record the breakdown of the wages. Once you have a broad idea of the value in your role, visit a salary comparison website confirm your search. Sites such as Paysa, LinkedIn, Salary, and PayScale are all great choices. For this particular example, we will use Salary.com as a demo. Once you visit the site, you will see a section titled "Know Your Worth." There you can get an estimate of your salary based on the job title and zip code.

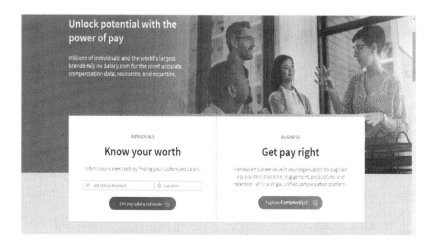

Type in your respective job title and you'll be required to select three different types of jobs for comparison. I want to go ahead and compare the difference in salary from a Financial Analyst I, II and III. You'll then be guided to a screen that describes the jobs you've selected, and this is where you'll have the option to obtain your salary data based on clicking "Free Salary Data" at the bottom. You'll be presented with a dashboard that highlights your salary range based on your selection criteria.

Again, there are a lot of factors that determine your salary so do not take this number as the end-all-be-all. Use it as a framework for understanding your market value with concrete data. Often, your university may have already done all of this work for you. Visit your Career Services Office or your Career Director and ask them if they know the market value for someone with your major and the role you're vying for.

As you've come to understand your worth in the market place, use this template to craft your strategy.

Thank you for agreeing to talk with me about the details of my compensation package. According to my research, a salary range for people doing this job in this area is from \$____ to \$____. Given my previous experience doing _____ (List your past accomplishment and the results the company gained from it), I believe this is a fair salary range for me in this position.

After you say this, relax and pause. What you may think is an uncomfortable tension filled moment, it is usually the time taken by the other person to consider your offer instead. Anything regarding money is always going to be an uncomfortable conversation so go into it knowing it's going to be awkward at times, and that's okay!

Once you've gathered your numbers and are having these conversations, you want to develop a strong negotiation strategy. Often, you may lose all your leverage when you're filling out a job application and it asks you for a range or salary requirements. It's crucial that you do your best to avoid discussing your salary and salary history until after you've received the offer. If an employer asks you to fill out that information in your job application, write "blank," "N/A," or "00000" to hold the conversation until you've received the offer.

Next, if an employer asks you to share your salary expectations during the interview, you can counter them with some of these responses:

"I'd like to learn a little bit more about the role before I set my salary expectations. As we move forward, I would hope that my salary is in line with the market rates for similar positions in this field."

"What is the salary range for this position with the workload you've described at this organization?"

"Before we discuss salaries, I would like to gain a little more understanding about your compensation strategy as well as the role and the results you're seeking. Can we hold that question for a bit?"

Sometimes, employers may also ask you to share your salary history. Here's a response to counter this dialogue:

"This position is not exactly the same as my previous jobs. I'd like to learn a little bit more about the role to determine a fair salary for this position."

As you continue with your dialogue, employers may rebut with the fact that you'll have future opportunities and to wait until next year. Your counter to this response:

"I believe I have demonstrated success with my previous experience and the confidence I have in my ability to translate it to this organization is well grounded. Because this number is a little lower than what I feel comfortable with, I believe that an additional amount in the range of $_____ to $____ would be fair."

If your employer still declines your counter-offer outright. Here's a suggested response:

"I appreciate your time. Are you able to elaborate on the reason behind the rejection?"

"Thank you for your time. I know that one most of the important assets in this role is the ability to _____ (insert a key indicator of success within this role that is quantitative from the previous question). If I'm able to deliver that _____ (insert time frame), would you be open to revisiting this conversation and raising my compensation to the range of _____ (insert target range)?

Thank you for your time. I know that one of the most important assets in this role is the ability to increase operational efficiency by 20% and limit our mistakes in the supply chain. If I'm able to deliver that result by the end of this quarter, would you be open to revisiting this conversation and raising my compensation to the range of $66,000 to $72,000?

Thank you for your time. I know that one of the most important assets in this role is the ability to communicate efficiently with our customers and increase our positive survey response rates by 15%. If I'm able to deliver that result by the end of this quarter, would you be open to revisiting this conversation and raising my compensation to the range of $5,000 to $10,000?

As a general rule of thumb, it is acceptable to ask for a 10% to 20% increase in your current base pay. Your confidence in this ask just comes from your research to support your argument.

Now if your employer has countered with an actual offer, but it is still not the number you were hoping for, here's a counter:

"Okay, if you can move the needle to get me to the range closer to $_____ to $_____ higher, I will sign **today**."

A guest on our podcast on *Episode 6: Negotiating Your Salary,* shares the power of now, especially in the world of business. It's the idea that your willingness to act in that moment will create the framework for both parties to move forward with the discussion.

Now, if they get back to you and say, "This is as high as we can possibly go for a position like this," consider the negotiation for a higher salary to have ended. Remember that compensation doesn't just include salary. Once you've reached this point, and you think you should still get a little more, feel free to ask about the opportunity for a sign-on-bonus, stipend to subsidies move-in costs, work from home, tuition reimbursement, higher PTO, etc.

The most important aspect to this whole thing are the niceties and respect your show the other party. You are not making demands, and you are not telling them what to do. It is a conversation and you should treat it as such. As you can see in our examples, phrases like, "Do you mind if," "I would appreciate it if," and "Thank you for your time" make this a courteous conversation as opposed to a strong list of demands.

CHAPTER 8

Owning the Internship/Job

Internships are like the first week of your freshman year. Anywhere you walk, you look like you're lost. You say hi to anyone you meet, and desperately try to remember the names of the people in your classes so you have someone to get your notes from for when you "accidentally" sleep past your 8 A.M.

Useless advice: **"Crush your internship."**

You've made your resume, completed several rounds of interviews, negotiated the perfect salary, and now you're walking through the front doors for your first day on the job. The reason why this chapter applies to both your internship and your job is that these are the things you should be doing in your first three months upon joining any organization, regardless of your role coming in as either an intern or a full-time hire. Now we're not just describing the job you want to do for the rest of your life, but these tips can be applied to your job as a lifeguard, cashier or a part-time campus job.

PRE

Now let's go back to right after you accept your offer. Don't just wait around until your first day to show initiative. Reach out to your soon-to-be manager if you know who it's going to be and ask them if there's anything you can do in the meantime to get ready to provide value to them immediately. Here is an example:

Also, reach out to some people at the company that you may be working with. When you start taking these small initiatives, others will you perceive you and your brand as a go-getter and you could be given bigger opportunities as soon as you step foot in that door on your very first day. Now, if the employer says to hold off until your first day to start doing the actual work, no problem! Use this idle time to meet as many people in the office via a quick phone call or a video meeting.

Here's an example of this conversation:

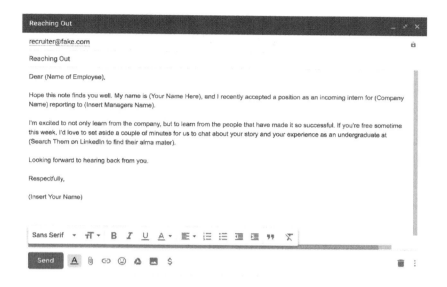

Refer back to the networking chapter on ways to handle these conversations.

As you're networking with the people in your office, utilize the time you have to brush up on any specialized skills the job requires such as a specific coding language, obtaining a certification, and staying up to date with industry news. A simple way to stay ahead of the pack is to set up Google News Alerts on your phone. Go to google.com/alerts in your browser and enter your company as the topic you want to track. Then, select, "Create Alert." Google now will notify you whenever the search engine finds a page that matches your company name.

Day Before Internship

Barring any unexpected emergencies, showing up late is never okay, especially on your first day of work. Therefore, make sure you know where you're going on your first day. Drive the route the day before and familiarize yourself with the traffic pattern. Also, just as you did for the interview, check Waze to see how the traffic is going to be at the time you'll be traveling that route. This will alleviate some of those first-day jitters.

First Day

Be the communication advocate. Just like in the interview, make sure to introduce yourself and smile. The stronger of a connection you build with these interns/coworkers, the more you'll be able to count on them throughout your time there and possibly even build lifelong friends.

Rishav's story about meeting up with UA people all the time.

Rishav on developing relationships with co-workers:

During my time at Under Armour, the first few days were always exhilarating simply because you're meeting so many people all at once. I can vividly recall putting myself out there initially to invite people over for dinner, contribute to the group chat and provide a helping hand whenever needed. That was in 2017, but that small act led to my finding some of my closest friends that I still keep in touch with today.

So, start those group chats, and people will gravitate towards you as the leader who's not afraid to put themselves out there. Full-time employees of the company will also see this, and you'll come across as a leader to them as well. Also do this if this is your first day as a full-time employee in the training class; same things apply here as well.

Get a tour from the administrative assistant, make them your best friend. Also consider staying late the first day to walk around and learn room names.

That night, look up co-workers on Facebooks and LinkedIn to get their names down. There's no sweeter sound to someone than their own name.

First Week

Your laptop's being set up, so go shadow someone who does your role because it'll be a good time to learn something and make a connection. If you're just sitting around, get used to company jargon on their website. Introduce yourself to the people around your cubicle.

Say "Hi, I'm (insert name). Do you mind if I shadow you for a little to see what you do?" or "Is there anything special that helped you when you first started?"

Goal-setting in those first weeks is crucial for a successful, outcome-driven experience. Set realistic goals for yourself with your manager, since they may have a better frame of reference for what you have time for. Don't over promise and under deliver; this is one of the worst things you can do. Another way to approach this might also be to learn what your main role is first and get a bit of a grasp on it so that you'll have a better sense of how much free time you'll have to pursue other projects.

For other projects, find ways to solve company issues. If a company uses an Excel spreadsheet, there is always a way to make it better. Learn a little VBA via YouTube and then apply it to decrease time spent searching within the spreadsheet or by automating calculations done repetitively. Another easy way to provide instant value is to create resources that future interns will be able to use to learn their role faster and lower the learning curve. This could include a Vizio flow diagram or a few paragraphs about where to find rooms, questions you had during your time there, or relevant co-workers and how they impacted your work. The best thing you can add to your resume leaving your internship is a story about how you made a company more efficient.

For each project, make a stakeholder map. People really appreciate being asked about their opinion and you'll save time on the back end by knowing the holistic view of your task. You should also keep relevant stakeholders in the loop regarding your timeline for the project and any road blocks that pop up keeping you from delivering on time.

Alex on Managing Stakeholders

I decided to create a workflow diagram for my position to help future people doing the task. I got to the end of the internship, two weeks away from our final presentations, and talked with a manager who sat a few cubicles down. I told him about what I was doing, and he asked me if I considered how it might impact other departments there. I had not! I went back and then added it into the flow. Make sure you know the scope of everyone your work might impact from the get-go. Do this by asking the heads of other departments if you work applies to them at all.

This will already start you off in their good books and also provide you with the ability to get a jump-start on those first weeks. This is especially important if you're reading this for an internship, as you are only there for a short time.

You'll be emailing a lot of people you don't know for work. Emailing etiquette: start with formal greetings, "Dear Mr., Ms., Director," but then if and when they invite you to use their first name, go with that and don't look back. Obviously if they introduce themselves of the bat with the first name then go with that.

Three-question rule: you're going to have a ton of questions. What the three-question rule allows you to do is build up some time between asks which keeps you from interrupting a colleague too much. A lot of times you'll also find that by the time you get to the third question, you will have found the answer to your first one. Also, spread the questions among co-workers, this keeps you from taking too much time from anyone and also allows you to get to know more people in the office.

Get to know and provide value to the administrative and executive assistants. Without being a kiss-up, bring them coffee and always greet them by their name on the way in and out of the office. They are the key-holders for the executives and decision makers. They also usually know the most about anyone and will be an invaluable resource to yourself all the way from knowing your way around the office to learning how to schedule a room in Outlook.

Email Directory - If your company gives you contacts for everyone in the company, utilize it! Find common ground based on university (used LinkedIn to do this research) and ask to meet with them to learn from their experiences. Now if they have a project and could use an intern's help, you will pop into their heads.

Alex on Building Stories

The most meaningful bullet points I took from my internships were from the projects outside of my main role. If you're not getting the experience you want, network around the company until you know someone who can get you that experience.

Moving Forward

Balance yourself, go to happy hours, go to basketball outside of work. Informal settings allow people to break down the barriers and also show your ability to hold yourself well in a social setting. Companies want you to still be a good person after leaving work as well so make sure to hold respect and not drive conversations towards topics that might make people uncomfortable – the obvious, sex, drugs, and politics. Now these are okay to talk about once brought up by a colleague; in fact, the ability to handle these conversations once brought up shows that you can be respectful and a great listener even when it comes to controversial topics.

The networking notepad. Every single person you meet, write down their name and three facts about them. It helps you to shine through as a caring member of the team/company. Fellow interns will begin to look up to you as the person who knows everyone.

Keep a weekly log where you can keep track of the projects you worked on, the tasks you performed, and the knowledge you gained. This includes learning lunches with colleagues, meetings, presentations, actual work you performed, etc. At the end of each week include goals for the following week.

Be a team player; if your team is staying late at work, you should too. Find a way to help them based on your skillset or be the research person.

Networking at the communal coffee pot. Introduce yourself to anyone else there or people that pass by. You'll see people here that might not sit in your immediate space. This is a great way to meet people on other teams and learn about other experiences within the company.

Alex on Networking Your Way to Experience

I introduced myself to someone who worked on the project management team, and by asking a few questions about what he did, he saw that I was interested and asked if I wanted to work with him on something to get experience in this area.

Ask your manager to sit in on the meetings they sit in on. These are where you can learn how these decisions are made. Whether to sit at the big table or on the side? If other interns who have been in the meetings before sit on the side, then follow suit but when unsure, sit at the big table to act like you belong. It shows you take yourself seriously but just make sure you're not taking an important stakeholder's chair. If you really want to play it safe just ask your manager or someone else you meet in the meeting.

How to dress, follow company culture but with a slight upgrade. Don't overdress too much or underdress because you'll stick out from company culture. Why we recommend up-dressing a little? Think about an airplane pilot. They could wear sweatpants in the cockpit and it wouldn't really make a difference whether or not the plane gets to its decision. A pilot knows how to fly a plane regardless of the pants he's wearing. It does, however, give the passengers comfort in knowing that someone who pays attention to the details of their clothing also probably pays attention in the cockpit. People take you more seriously if you're dressed nicer. Now once you've provided a ton of value and people at work know you and the great work you provide, then feel free to adjust to what you want your brand to be.

Getting stuck in a position you don't like. Network early on to prevent being stuck later on. If people know your passions, they'll look for ways to fit you based on that. You also don't know what's possible until you know what other people at the company do.

Alex on a Game Time Change

I had a colleague who came into a super technical position and hated it. Her boss wouldn't let her move to other parts within the company simply from her asking. She had, however, networked with someone in the project management office who reached out to her boss on behalf of her to seek extra help with a project. Her boss agreed and within a few weeks she was a full time intern in the project management office.

"Can I buy you lunch," the magic phrase. Who doesn't want a free meal. I've also come to realize that nine out of ten times you'll end up getting a free lunch. Now, we would strongly advise against using this method simply to get free lunches because this will become obvious at some point and you'll also come across as disingenuous. What we're saying is that it's something you should do to get to know people at the company. Taking the time to desire to learn about others' backgrounds and experience will give them a good frame of mind for you being someone who wants to learn and grow. All the above applies as well in terms of learning more about positions you may want to try, doing better in your own role since you know how it impacts them, or even just having a support group.

Send an email saying something like, "Dear Person, I've heard your name tossed around as someone who's really good at doing X here, and I wanted to see if you had time for me to buy you lunch and learn from your experiences with the company and any tips for how you've been able to succeed."

Another important part of the internship or job is learning to crave and act on criticism that's been given to you. Don't take criticism personally; however, do make it a personal responsibility to ensure that whoever's given it to you sees your growth in that area.

Alex on Taking Criticism

I was tasked with presenting a piece of technology I built for a higher-level executive and completely botched it. I knew it, they knew it, so I asked for ways I could improve my technical demos moving forward. They advised me to focus more on the outcomes of what the tool performed which I made sure to incorporate during my next presentation. One of my last days there, they pulled me aside one on one and pointed to my ability to grow as a reason for wanting to bring me back full-time.

Always take criticism seriously, and if it's not given, ask for it. A good way to do this is to set up weekly or bi-weekly checkpoints with your manager to review the work you're doing and asking for any ways you can improve.

Congratulations, you've successfully made it through the three months of your internship or first three months of your job. Get your managers to look over what you've added to your resume. Ask them if they have any numbers to add to what you've done that'll help you prove your value later. If you're in your full-time position and your first three months have just been training, wait until you get settled into your full-time role and then make sure to reach out regarding how you can word the value you're providing. As an intern, also use your resume here to network around. Since these are experienced professionals who've probably hired many people they will able to give you great feedback and suggestions for improving it. As we've mentioned earlier, by doing this they also now have a stake in your resume and can vouch for the work you've done. They may also be able to provide you with validating numbers or other areas of impact that you've had.

Final Presentations

Practice your presentations. Book out the room night before. Don't memorize what you're saying.

All of your hard work is now coming together for the executives, directors, managers, and your fellow peers to see. As you're getting started, we're sure you're feeling overwhelmed by the type of content you should be sharing. Therefore, to make this step easier for you, we suggest you journal your activities daily or weekly as you can reference back to these documents once the time comes i.e., now.

When planning your topic, you have to assess your audience's knowledge of what you've worked on. A presentation isn't for you to have a one-way dialogue, but rather to collaboratively inform. So, ask yourself, for the people attending, what do they know about this topic and what do they not know? It's simple, but starting with this framework can help you craft a story that your audience can relate to. This is where you can ask your mentors, colleagues and managers on their familiarity of the topic you've chosen to highlight and present on. For instance, if there are Vice Presidents and Directors in attendance, are they aware of the problem that existed prior to a solution that you implemented? If not, address the main point first when crafting your story. Lastly, always think in terms of your audience's shoes. What's in it for them? What do they gain by being there? What are some of their values that you're adhering to? To create this list, read through the company's five-year strategy plan, their one-page business plan and lastly, talk to your mentors about the executives' likes and dislikes when someone is giving them a presentation.

Now that you have an idea about your audience, it's time to start creating the story! To start, find a time to sit down and make a list of all the possible pieces of information that you would like to share pertaining to your topic. Now, think back to your audience. Based on their understanding of the topic and the information you've presented, what areas of conversations will they find most valuable? Narrow your choices from here and aim for efficiency in information. As you start thinking about your introduction, things such as posing a question, highlighting a large statistic, or broadcasting a counter-intuitive message are all bound to get attention. From there, you want to quickly describe the current scenario, the tasks and actions you took to move the needle along, and lastly, the results that came about from your solution. This framework is similar to that of a STAR framework from the behavioral interview chapter. In the end, once it's all said and done, what should your audience know after attending the presentation?

In terms of creating your slides, find a slide deck that is aesthetically pleasing. Do not use a basic PowerPoint template that's been utilized for the millionth time. You can also ask your manager or your mentor to get access to a list of company slide decks to utilize. If you have room for options, Google "Free PowerPoint Pitch Decks" to get a list of amazing slides to use for free! Once you're happy with a slide that works for you, start typing, but start typing short sentences or simple words to convey your message. Never write full sentences or long paragraphs and read them directly from the slide. This is a waste of everyone's time. When it comes to highlighting data, think of the message you're trying to convey and what the lasting impression of the audience might be. If you want them to feel shocked, highlighting your data set and using bold colors such as black and red are great uses of what you want them to focus on.

Lastly, now comes time for the delivery. The audience focus should be on you. By delivering your content with large gestures, maintaining eye contact, and leaning towards the audience during certain inflection points, you're establishing a connection. This is where it might be best to go through a couple of dry runs with your colleagues and friends before the big day. The day before, book the same room and practice in that room. Your familiarity will help your nerves stay calm and collected. However, your familiarity with the room and the content should not mean that you memorize the entire presentation. In your head, use a couple of keywords to jog your memory and let it flow naturally. With practice, also comes preparation. Preparation for the inevitable faults with technology. Print out a couple of backup copies of your presentation just in case the network goes down and go with the flow. Remember, you've already done all the hard work; the delivery is the easy part!

Some final notes as you wrap up your time there:

Leave written thank you cards. It's how you get remembered. Buy a set of 20 from a local grocery store for $5; it's absolutely worth it. You should write one to anyone who's spent time meeting with you, guided you through a project, assisted you with an issue.

Dear Person,

Thank you so much for the time you've taken these past few months to get me acquainted with the company and learn from your personal growth and experiences. (Include a personal sentence about their life to show you care.) I wish both your kids, Sam and Sarah, the best as they begin their first year of college and high school. Just let them know that from someone who personally struggled to find their identity, those can be great years to try new things and explore new passions.

Warmest Regards,
Your Name

Expressing Desire to Come Back

This one may sound simple if you enjoyed your internship, but so many people forget to initiate the conversation with your hiring directors and managers. Once the internship is coming to an end, simply state, "I've thoroughly enjoyed my time here and I've seen myself grow personally and professionally. I'd love the opportunity to come back and would love to discuss next steps moving forward."

A final note: Be nice to everyone you meet and make the IT people your best friends. Just trust us on this one.

Outro

You've got framework now to (or you've not got the framework to depending on what legal guy says).

- Set your SMART goals by keeping your head out of the clouds,

- Become the VP of something at some organization you joined after finding your passion from something you read,

- Build a network of many recruiters before you needed the job by asking for advice on your resume,

- Make a killer resume, a LinkedIn profile that reflects that of a young and passionate professional, and write that cover letter that's going to get you through the gatekeeper by focusing on wording your experiences by task, what you learned, and the impact you had,

- Attend the local career fair and walk away with an interview for tomorrow since you showed how interested you were in the position applying online beforehand,

- Interview like a champ by knowing your core value stories,

- Turn your internship into a full-time position or full-time position into a promotion by networking around the office,

- Add an extra $5,000 to your salary by using the power of now.

Congratulations, you're a young professional. Look, this stuff isn't something that happens overnight, and we're not shying away from telling you that its difficult. You will run into your own unique set of challenges as you progress through your own experiences, but there is nothing to lose by seeking feedback and fostering self-improvement. The best conversations we've had are the ones where our goals, vision and strategies were challenged. Although that might sound intimidating, it actually cuts down on the time you would've spent figuring it out on your own and moves you closer towards that job! If you would like personalized help applying any of the above chapters to your unique situation, we'd love to help.

Visit www.PracticallyPassionate.com to get personalized help, find the podcast, and get access to our personal resume and cover letter templates. The podcast can also be found on Spotify, Apple Podcasts, and SoundCloud. You can also reach us via e-mail at info@practicallypassionate.com

Here are a few notes from people we've helped:

"It doesn't get much easier than this. It's one thing to hear about jobs, networking, interviewing, etc. from people that have spent years in an industry. It's another to hear advice from peers who have seen "success" by navigating through the system." ~ **Madhav, Emerging Leaders Associate, Technology Track at Nielsen**

જ્જ ✄

"Earlier this semester, when I had an interview, I sat down with Practically Passionate for about an hour to prep. They helped me curate the most perfect answers to showcase my experience AND to make me one of the most competitive candidates. Needless to say, I got the job! Thanks, Practically Passionate!"~ **Zini, Intern at Ingersoll Rand**

"Thanks to Practically Passionate, I got my first interview ever." ~ **Omar, Graduating Senior**

જ્જ ✄

"I walked into my interview incredibly confident since I knew how to leverage my stories for the interview questions." ~ **Honji, International Student studying here in the U.S.**

ॐ ॐ

"I have been looking for someone to help me with my resume and LinkedIn and every time I get the same feedback "structure is good, grammar is good etc.", even from my technical English professor. This is the first time in a long time I got valuable help, not so much on the common things, but on the personality and values that my resume embodies." ~ **Yasmine, Computer Science Major**

ॐ ॐ

As a senior in college that had no previous internship experience, finding a company that would hire me felt like a needle in a haystack, however after receiving some consulting advice from Rishav and Alex, I was able to land a full-time position. I could not have done it without these two; these guys really know what they're doing! ~ **Christopher, Graduating Senior**

Made in the USA
Middletown, DE
14 December 2018